Choosing to Engage

The Scaffle method: Practical steps for purposeful
stakeholder engagement

Rebecca Dahl
with a special collaboration section by Dr Mark Elliott

STARLING
BOOKS

First published in 2018 by Starling Books

an imprint of Collabforge, Melbourne, Australia
© Collabforge, 2018

collabforge

Cover design by Peter Reardon
Interior design by Mariela Schultz
Printed in Australia by IngramSpark

NATIONAL LIBRARY OF AUSTRALIA

A catalogue record for this book is available from the National Library of Australia

ISBN: 9780648439806 (paperback)
ISBN: 9780648439813 (e-book)

Contents

Introduction

The role of stakeholder engagement in policy and service delivery

The Australian public's *trust* in government is at an all-time low.

Only 26% of us trust government to work in our interest, and our trust in democracy is at its lowest level – 60% – since 1979 (Cameron & McAllister, 2016). These statistics doubtless infuriate anyone working hard for the common good in government, often in stressful and difficult circumstances. While some contributing factors regarding these numbers are difficult to influence, greater involvement of the public in decision-making is one aspect where immediate improvement is possible. Better stakeholder engagement can help rebuild the relationship between the citizens and the state, reducing risk and saving money at the same time.

Poorly done stakeholder engagement can have significant financial and reputational costs, similar to or worse than not doing engagement at all (Clarke, 2015). A bad experience can leave citizens, other stakeholders and policy professionals hesitant to engage again, reinforcing the knee-jerk reaction of only doing the minimum necessary consultation, and turning engagement into a tedious box-ticking exercise.

However, when done well, engagement can build enormous trust by improving transparency and enabling stakeholders to influence, or at least understand, the decisions that will most affect them. It also allows policy-makers to make better policy, ultimately making more effective use of the public purse. Beyond simply being a way to avoid or mitigate negative responses, authentic engagement – at the right time, and in the right way – can lead to policy and service outcomes that stand up to scrutiny and the test of time.

What problem are we solving?

Engagement – whether with the public, subject-matter experts, or other policy experts – is a fundamental part of the role of any public servant engaged in policy-making, program development or service delivery. But it is a topic that tends to receive little focus in formal training. Policy-makers and planners are adept communicators and highly diplomatic relationship builders, and these skills naturally lend themselves to engagement at all levels. However, with most learning about engagement being done on the job, gaps in capability naturally occur.

At the same time, engagement (in the form of consultation), particularly at higher levels of government, is most often viewed as a tool to mitigate risk rather than improve outcomes for citizens. This means that incoming public servants are trained to further embed old-world thinking about the role of engagement. In order to embrace the opportunities engagement can provide, we need to build the capability of public servants, and learn how to use innovative and more participatory engagement techniques in a way that doesn't conflict with risk appetite.

Open-government movements are championing the potential for involving a wide range of stakeholders in policy and program design, and for more transparency in decision-making. However, the aspirational improvements promised by prior research and the recommendations of government 2.0 and open-government strategies[1] are currently hampered by an all-or-nothing worldview and theory-based advice. This particularly applies when the recommendations are made in a way that implies one way (collaboration) is 'better' than another (consultation). Collaborative approaches, applied in the right way, can profoundly improve outcomes. However, consultation has played, and will continue to play, an important role in governance.

Through our collective experience at Collabforge of more than 23 years of working with government, we have found that public servants are naturally inclined to work passionately in the best interests of the public. But the environment they work within is often risk-averse. This makes radical change virtually impossible to achieve. We believe that, instead of aspirational, theory-based advice, we should provide a practical, outcomes-based approach to improving engagement and transparency – one that is easy to apply and ultimately has a big impact on public perception.

This book focuses on making better use of engagement activities as a complement to current practice. Through the strategic use of specific types of engagement techniques, and by addressing issues of transparency where possible, the shift to a more participatory style of government will be a more gentle and natural one.

---

1 These are initiatives that work to improve the dialogue between government and external groups in a more participatory and transparent manner.

A different approach to engagement planning

Planning good public engagement involves a mix of art and science, but it's more common sense than rocket engineering. During research undertaken by our team at Collabforge, we discovered some simple concepts that are often overlooked. By combining these with our own experience, we have been able to create effective methods that will give a big boost to your engagement outcomes.

In this book, we will explore:

- » what engagement is, and its benefits
- » the consequences of poor engagement
- » what is being done today and how this can be improved upon.

We then complement the theory with step-by-step methods to:

- » plan strategically for engagement throughout a policy or service design process
- » design an individual engagement activity
- » deliver better collaborative engagements, and determine when you should and shouldn't use them.

We've also included a reference guide to 35 different activities you can use to plan your next stakeholder engagement (see Part Four; page 97).

Scaffle – digital stakeholder engagement support

This book articulates a number of concepts that we've baked into our digital product, Scaffle. You can use this book on its own or as a complement to the application. It is not intended as a user guide – both book and application can stand alone. But it can be helpful to understand the theory, even if a tool takes care of some of the implementation for you.

The Scaffle application is a product under development by the team at Collabforge, funded by the Australian Government's Business Research and Innovation Initiative (BRII). Scaffle's core innovation is a guided process that combines flexible templates with smart recommendations, to help users create better engagement plans that are aligned with the cycles of policy-making and service delivery. It can significantly reduce your planning time and the need for external advice, preserving budget for professionals to assist with delivery instead. It can also lower risk by providing better record-keeping, quickly generate reports on the state of your engagement project, and help you give better feedback to participants at the end of your project.

You simply tell Scaffle about the key details of an engagement you're planning and the platform will recommend a plan, with rounds of engagement, activities, and links to providers and tools. It will also connect you to learning modules and training opportunities. Scaffle is designed to integrate with existing engagement methods and the digital platforms already in use.

Who is Collabforge?

Collabforge has a 10-year history of working with governments in Australia (and several abroad, including in Canada) to implement collaboration on policy and programs. As a niche consultant on collaboration and innovation, we are painfully aware of both the opportunities and the challenges faced by public servants when it comes to engagement.

In 2016 we responded to a BRII grant that challenged responders to develop approaches to making collaboration and consultation with the public better, broader and cheaper. The Scaffle digital application and the methodology outlined in this book are the outputs of our response to this grant. This work has been led by researcher and practitioner Rebecca Dahl, informed by Collabforge founder Dr Mark Elliott's PhD research on collaboration theory and practice. We hope it is of use to those starting their engagement practice and to experienced professionals alike. Many of the concepts will be familiar as aspects of practice, but we hope that the structured process we outline in the following sections will enable their better coordination and implementation.

1 Reframing stakeholder engagement

What is engagement?

For such a fundamental part of good governance, the definitions around the act of communicating, consulting and collaborating with the public and other stakeholders are surprisingly imprecise. Stakeholder engagement and consultation vary significantly in interpretation depending on the context. You probably have a gut feeling about what we mean by 'stakeholder engagement'. But now is a good time to clarify this, as the following sections of this book rely on a solid, shared understanding of a few key terms, 'engagement' in particular.

In the research Collabforge conducted to produce this book (see the upcoming section 'The current state of engagement in the Australian context' on page 18), we found that the term 'engagement' is used with great confidence but for differing purposes. To some, it means an ongoing process of almost daily conversations with external parties, proactively and reactively responding to issues of the day. For others, it has an internal focus – the conversations that occur within government or with influential stakeholders on policy or other matters. Different again is the definition embraced by many local governments that sees engagement as an outcome, 'achieved when the community is and feels part of the overall governance of that community' (Victorian Local Governance Association, 2018).

For our purposes, we wanted a term that describes the act of *involving* stakeholders in the task of creating or implementing policy and programs.

There are different ways of involving stakeholders, each of which enables them to have a specific level of influence on your outcome or process. These can be roughly grouped (with a degree of overlap) by the manner in which they influence or have an impact. We call this the 'mode of involvement', but you may be more familiar with the phrase 'level of participation'. Both are focused on modelling the manner of working with stakeholders in regards to the potential for influence or impact. Before we can define engagement, we need a shared understanding of these ways of involving stakeholders, as our definition must be inclusive of all modes of involvement.

Understanding modes of involvement

There are a number of frameworks that exist to help clarify potential modes of involvement and when to use them. Perhaps the best known is the IAP2's Public Participation Spectrum framework (IAP2 International Federation, 2014), which breaks involvement down into five modes on a spectrum of increasing levels of public impact:

Inform → Consult → Involve → Collaborate → Empower

While a number of more context-specific frameworks now exist, there's no denying that this framework has helped 'community engagement' become part of the public service vernacular, changing the perception of policy from something that is done to stakeholders, to something in which they can have a more participatory role (Ross, Baldwin & Carter, 2016).

In order to offer a tool that is more specific to the public service context, the Commonwealth Department of Industry, Innovation and Science recently produced a framework that includes modes of involvement, named The Australian Public Service Framework for Engagement and Participation (see Figure 1). This framework has four modes of involvement, described as 'ways the APS engages with the public': Share, Consult, Deliberate and Collaborate. These modes use grounding questions to help you decide which one is the most appropriate for your use case. This situational aspect, and the framework's specificity to the public sector, make it particularly applicable to engagement planning in Scaffle.

The Australian Public Service Framework for Engagement and Participation is the source of our definitions of the terms 'collaboration', 'consultation', 'deliberation' and 'sharing/communication', and how these relate to the concept of involvement. We will return to how modes of involvement can be helpful to your planning in Part Two (see page 37) of this book.

Figure 1: The Australian Public Service Framework for Engagement and Participation

Mode	Definition
SHARE 'Does government need to tell the public about a government initiative?'	When we are sharing information, communication is one-way, from the government to the public. People receive factual information to describe an event, new initiative or changes to an existing process. The promise: 'We will keep you informed'.
CONSULT 'Does government need to gather feedback from the public about a problem or proposed solution?'	When consulted, people are typically provided a link to a discussion paper proposing solutions to an identified and framed problem. They are then provided with an opportunity to weigh-in and provide input on the proposed solution within a given timeframe. Ideally, when provided with this opportunity to comment, participants' views and lived experiences should be supported with quantitative data or analysis. The promise: 'We will keep you informed, listen to and acknowledge concerns and aspirations, and provide feedback on how public input influenced the decision'.
DELIBERATE 'Does government need help from the public to frame or solve a problem?'	In a 'deliberate' engagement, people are asked to help identify an issue and/ or develop a strategy that the government commits itself to delivering. Participants discuss how to find common ground and collectively arrive at an agreement. Participants need to be able to support their lived experiences with evidence and facts. The promise: 'We will look to you for advice and innovation in formulating solutions and incorporate your advice and recommendations into the decisions to the maximum extent possible, subject to the boundaries and rules set by the engagement plan'.
COLLABORATE 'Does government need help from the public to find and implement a solution?'	In a 'collaborative' engagement, people work with the government to define an issue, and develop and deliver proposed solutions. Participants share decision-making and implementation of solutions. Again, participants need to be able to support their lived experiences with evidence and facts. The promise: 'We will look to you for advice and innovation in formulating solutions and incorporate your advice and recommendations into the decisions to the maximum extent possible, subject to the boundaries and rules set by the engagement plan. We will need your help to implement the solutions together'.

Source: © Department of Industry, Innovation and Science 2018, Discover phase report: Hidden in plain sight (Prototype stage report: Commitment 5.2 of Australia's first Open Government National Action Plan)

Why we can't use the term 'consultation'

The involvement of stakeholders, specifically when referring to the public, is most commonly understood throughout the public service as 'consultation'. However, as we've discussed, the term 'consultation' implies that the involvement will take a specific mode. It might be very familiar, but 'consultation' is too narrow a term to suit our purposes. Given this, we need to redefine the term 'engagement' to extend its definition to include all stakeholders and possible modes of involvement.

Our definition of engagement

Engagement is the act of involving stakeholders in the design and implementation of policy and programs, without limiting that participation to a specific mode. Stewart (2009, p. 13) states it quite well, explaining engagement as 'deliberate strategies for involving those outside government in the policy process. "Policy process", in this context, means ways of making policy decisions and ways of implementing them'.

One component of Stewart's definition is critical to how we will use the term 'engagement'. Specifically, it connects it to the policy process itself. Engagement is not separate to the processes it supplements but rather runs parallel to them, providing critical input and feedback at multiple points. And we include all potential stakeholders in engagement, not just those outside government. From the national stage to direct conversations with internal experts, all the stakeholders engaged have a role in the outcome, which should be acknowledged and planned for.

Evaluating engagement

Engagement itself speaks only to involvement, not to the quality or integrity of the process. To get to better engagement requires consideration of those who will be affected by the policy or program the engagement has informed, as well as those involved. 'Good' engagement can therefore be considered to have occurred if the participants and affected parties feel that the policy or service was created and implemented in a manner that was transparent and fair to the interests of all involved.

The benefits of good engagement

Political, social and economic factors all come into play during the process of making and implementing policy. Good engagement provides advantages that thread through all three. There are advantages for both politicians and public servants in being ahead of the emerging issues and concerns of constituents; in being able to improve the efficiency and cost-effectiveness of the policies being implemented; and in improving the state of democracy both for and in the eyes of the public. At its most basic, engagement does four things well:

» It enables access to information and the evidence needed for good decision-making.

» It lessens risk by broadening decision-making input.

» It provides new ideas that can break open 'wicked problems' by avoiding one-sided thinking.

» It builds public trust in government.

Improving research and evidence gathering

Engagement has an important role to play at the information-gathering and research stages of a policy-making process. Citizens and subject-matter experts are great sources of direct information, such as sentiment and data about current circumstances. They can help map local resources, specify risks, propose ideas, and potentially identify options for future implementation paths. While desktop research will always be coloured by the objectives of the researcher, direct engagement in the research stages enables you to ask project-specific questions and get the most relevant results possible.

In addition to raw data, stakeholders are a great source of qualitative and quantitative information references. For example, subject-matter experts may know of recent relevant studies that have been conducted. Likewise, citizens may be able to inform public servants if another department has recently approached them about similar issues. This can improve the efficiency and reach of the research by reducing unnecessary duplication.

Reducing risk

Risk plays a role both in why engagement is so important, and why the techniques most often selected are those that provide very little actual engagement with or between stakeholders. We think of these two types of risk as reputational risk and confrontational risk. These often share a correlation as the risk profile increases, but not always.

1. *Reputational risk*: the risk that your project/policy will backfire due to inadequate engagement

2. *Confrontational risk*: the risk that your engagement will turn sour due to inadequate planning or facilitation.

To engage with the least possible risk depends on a thorough analysis of stakeholder sentiment and the engagement of key stakeholders. When this is done well, stakeholders will feel that the policy or program is well suited to their needs and expectations.

While it's not possible to make everyone happy, at the very least, good engagement will leave you well prepared for any negative reactions, and ahead of the press. Neither politicians nor public servants particularly like a surprise or public backlash.

'Wicked' problem-solving

Wicked problems are defined as those issues that are particularly resistant to solutions from within government. This is usually due to their complexity – they are beyond the capability of any one agency to understand, suffer from differing opinions on causation, and require a broad range of stakeholders to be managed (Australian Public Service Commission, 2007). High-quality engagement offers the potential for public servants to better explore, understand and build solutions to wicked problems.

Wicked problems usually require solving at both the grassroots level and from the top down, in order to shift resistance. Engagement, particularly using collaborative techniques, can build coordinated and diverse solutions to these problems.

Rekindling public trust

Improving engagement, both in process and planning, presents a significant opportunity to recover positive public sentiment. When engagement works, opposition to new policies and programs is lessened, and the ability to work collaboratively with stakeholders in the implementation phase is improved. Few aspects of a policy-maker's role can have greater impact on success, in terms of both policy outcomes and delivering on the democratic promise, than good engagement. Being able to transparently communicate the basis of decisions – particularly the evidence, and the sources of information and feedback – creates a strong foundation on which to build the public's trust.

The consequences of poor engagement

Not doing engagement, or doing it poorly, can result in anything from a less-effective policy to a massive public scandal. Poor engagement will likely mean that:

» the policy or service fails in a way that was predictable and avoidable

» stakeholders are more antagonised after engagement than before it

» stakeholders do not believe in, or support, your final recommendations

» you waste time and/or resources without getting any meaningful engagement.

There is a great opportunity to be had in learning from past mistakes, and so this section will look at what can happen when engagement goes wrong.

Missing a key risk

Smart, systemic thinkers though they may be, policy-makers don't have all the answers. Engagement helps make sure that critical questions don't go unasked. It provides the best chance of finding weak spots and patching holes before a policy is finalised or a program launched. Without talking to experts or the people affected, it's easy to make assumptions that don't align with reality, or to miss opportunities and ideas.

However, despite this, many policies and programs are developed and decided without significant engagement, particularly in the early stages. According to research conducted by Collabforge, 70% of engagements occur after the options for a policy have already been decided. And half of these provide only a single recommended option. This means that their focus is on identifying last-minute risks, rather than sourcing better solutions or checking that the right problems are being solved. As a result, the policy or service may not be as effective or efficient as it could be, or critical inherent risks may be missed. While this may take years to emerge and be less important at the political level, it will eventually come back to make the lives of public servants more difficult.

Case study: The ill-fated Home Insulation Project

In early 2009, the then prime minister of Australia, Kevin Rudd, announced a $42 billion Nation Building and Jobs Plan that included an ill-fated program that became known as the Home Insulation Project (HIP). The HIP tasked the housing industry with creating more jobs for low-skilled workers while delivering improvements to the energy efficiency of new and existing buildings.

The program commenced with two public servants being tasked over a long weekend to develop a policy proposal, with specific instructions 'not to contact industry and not to speak to colleagues'. From its announcement in February, there were only five short months in which to develop and begin to implement this program. Consultation occurred only in regards to the announced policy, and even in the development phases this remained limited, with a group of four ministers overseeing and making decisions dominated by political imperatives rather than industry concerns.

The speed and dominance of political interests, rather than a codesigned and engagement-centric approach from the outset, caused a myriad issues, from a failure to invite key industry members (electricity industry representatives) and organise early consultation sessions, to a general lack of understanding of the complexities and challenges that would be faced.

A royal commission later conducted to investigate deaths arising from the program, and misuse of the funds put into it, found that the lack of a proper and accountable deliberative process, combined with poor risk planning, were critical elements of the project's ultimate termination. Had industry been invited to be part of a transparent codesign process for the policy from the outset, the outcome could have been very different. (Summary based on Shergold, 2015.)

Participants are more angry/frustrated/disengaged after engagement than before it

It's not uncommon for engagement to actually make relationships with stakeholders worse if it isn't planned or communicated well. This can be caused by inexperience in running a particular technique, not understanding the needs of your stakeholders, or failing to test or design your engagement with at least one person who represents or knows your stakeholders well.

Misalignment between the involvement mode promised to participants and their real ability to influence an outcome is a common source of frustration. For example, collaborative-style engagement activities are attractive to well-intentioned public servants because they present an opportunity to get those affected onside by giving them a role in the solving of their own problem. However, they require careful planning and the authority to enable participants to influence the outcome. This is why they are often best used to help in the early stages, when you can promise they will influence the issues raised, or plan for your engagement, rather than when making decisions about an outcome. If these processes are run in a way in which they become a consultative exercise rather than a collaborative one, frustrations are likely to emerge.

A common scenario is where the first part of an activity focuses on open ideation, letting participants think they are designing a solution, but the prioritisation step then introduces predetermined options, not those the group created. This leaves participants feeling that their time has been wasted and their ideas are not valued. Most people involved in these failed collaborations comment that they would rather have been told up-front what influence they would have, so they could adjust their expectations accordingly. It's not necessarily the lack of influence that they have a problem with, more the lack of honesty and transparency. They feel frustrated, negative towards the resultant policy, and uninterested in being involved in the future.

Case study: A failure to connect with stakeholders

In the very early days of Collabforge, we became involved in a project to develop a website which was to serve the needs of a range of stakeholders. To help determine these needs, the brief for the website, and make sure all the stakeholders felt like they had a hand in the outcome, we brought together all the stakeholders for a day of collaboration to codesign the website. However, at that point in time, we were inexperienced at communicating the purpose and managing expectations for collaborative participation. At the same time, this group of stakeholders, having senior roles in a primary industry and were not as responsive to being offered a new way of working as other, more innovative groups had been previously. This came to a head at the point in the workshop when we asked them to participate more actively by showing us prototype designs, instead of 'telling' us what they wanted. They felt like they had already provided everything that we needed to know, and now we were wasting their time. This devolved the group dynamic to a point where there was a risk of damaging our client's relationship with their stakeholders. While this was thankfully avoided, the project was irrevocably affected.

Unknown to us we had made two common, and related mistakes. We had failed to clearly communicate the reason for our approach in bringing the group together, and at the same time, set up a power dynamic where we were perceived to be in the role of the "servant" to the stakeholder "master". They assumed that we were there to do a job for them and treated us as such. Meanwhile, our intention had been to establish a working relationship between them, whereby we might facilitate and action items, where they would also work with each other and us to determine and distribute tasks such as content creation or design decisions. If we had more carefully conducted a stakeholder mapping or risk analysis, we might have determined that deeper collaboration and cocreation with this group was probably not something that could be achieved in a half day workshop. Particularly not on a project or issue that participants didn't feel a strong sense of urgency on.

Participants do not connect with, or support, your recommendations

Related to the point above, another common source of frustration for participants is a lack of feedback about how their input was used. Without some sort of report – either bundling responses or providing individual comments – it is impossible for participants to know if their hard work was even read. While the reasons for not taking the advice might be perfectly valid, this is not made transparent without providing the necessary feedback. Participants are much less likely to support your recommendations if they feel that their voices have been ignored.

Case study: Projection of political abuse and corruption

In early 2016, the newly elected government of Newfoundland and Labrador launched an engagement project, 'Our Fiscal Future', to seek solutions to the Canadian province's financial problems. The initial public response to the planned engagement was less than optimistic. A number of articles were written pointing to an abject lack of commitment or evidence of any mechanism to utilise public response in policy. Jon Parsons (2016) went so far as to suggest that the government already had austerity plans in place and that the consultation was an attempt to ensure that when the public responded negatively, the government could defend itself by saying: 'You asked for it'.

The provincial budget that was released after the engagement in late 2016 caused a wave of protest and unrest. Evidence from a member of the governing party at the time has since revealed that the process of creating the budget involved no internal consultation, not even from the party's own district representatives, and that Cabinet members alone did the decision-making (Parsons, 2016). The original engagement website also makes no reference to how the outputs affected the decision process (Government of Newfoundland and Labrador, 2018). This made it especially hard for the public to believe that the government legitimately took the results of the engagement into consideration.

It's impossible to know the degree to which the engagement influenced the budget, whether the public outcry was inevitable given the cuts required, or if a better process might have led to a more tempered outcome. The only clear fact is that the budget deficit seems to have continued to grow (Atlantic Business Magazine, 2018), despite various promises and the reality that seniors, families and rural communities have been disproportionately affected by the cuts (Rollmann, 2016). Because the cuts seem to be in opposition to the concerns of citizens, they have fuelled accusations of unfair treatment and the political abuse of power. This highlights both the challenges in measuring the quality of engagement, and how poor communication can make a bad situation worse.

You don't get any useable feedback

Engagement with participants is by no means guaranteed. If a consultation paper is simply posted to the internet along with communications to key groups, it is unlikely to get a response. Likewise, if an engagement is poorly communicated, participants may not understand their stake in the outcomes and take the time to respond. A consultation activity without responses is almost worse than not consulting at all, as it will have been a complete waste of time and resources.

On the flip side, a poorly thought out engagement activity may be met with responses that are unuseable. A lack of framing or misworded questions can force respondents to interpret how to respond for themselves, and what they arrive at may not be what you thought you were asking for. If it emerges that you didn't use any of the responses you received because you'd designed your engagement badly, this could put you in a difficult situation.

Case study: Unintentionally reinforcing social inequality

In South Africa, water management has been a key issue of concern in addressing many of the inequalities between cultural groups. The participation of local people was a guiding principle of reforms commencing in the early 90's. Central to this concept of participation was the need to 'redress of imbalances of power' (Wilson & Perret, 2010, p. 326), in addition to the belief that a sense of ownership would contribute to the more sustainable management of the resource. Early efforts in this respect, however, saw the inequalities deepen rather than improve. Research in this area has concluded that misdesigned engagement efforts were a contributing factor. Some of the causes identified were:

Claims of representation: An issue that commonly occurs is where members of one marginalised group are given a voice to speak for other members whom they claim (or are perhaps assumed) to represent, but who in actuality they do not represent. This was highlighted in relation to South Africa by the findings of Naidoo (2009), who showed that even though the importance of women as the primary users and managers of water in rural households was widely acknowledged, their representation in planning and decision-making was very low. Furthermore, at participatory events they attended, they did not actively take part in discussions. This inequality was reinforced by those in power, for whom the need to show quick project outcomes led to a dismissal of the importance of working to give a voice to this group, instead assuming that the participation they had secured would be enough. In extreme cases, this can lead to compensation being given to a corrupt individual (such as a village chief) for infrastructure works, rather than to those whom the works will most significantly affect (Wilson & Perret, 2010, p. 330).

Bias of purpose: In participating, there was a clear outcome for both the researchers and the institutions commissioning the work. The former would receive payment and credit for completing their work. The latter would meet their obligations and secure further funding. Both outcomes would be achieved regardless of whether or not the engagement process was done in a way that was fair, equitable, and achieved better outcomes for those they were engaging with. A clear outcome for the engaged groups was lacking because the mandate was engagement itself. Larger, more-organised bulk water users, such as white farmers and industry, could ensure that they had their needs met. However, individuals without power, or knowledge of the language or maths required to understand the material being decided on, were put at a severe disadvantage. Put in these terms, it is easy to see why so many engagements end in frustration for participants but good case studies for government.

Poorly chosen or delivered engagement methods: Analysis of the engagements undertaken showed that, because the participatory programs were fundamentally designed to fulfil policy requirements and/or provide a channel of influence for key, highly vocal stakeholders, there was no incentive to seek out methods or design for the involvement of disadvantaged or marginalised community members. For example, in many cases, the practitioners designing and running the participatory activities did not speak the local language. This created immediate separation and a lack of trust of the facilitators, even though interpreters were used at the events. Visual displays of data were too complicated to be understood and to enable adequate discussion, because those creating the material didn't test it with participants (Naidoo, 2009). In one example, the water management proposal was published in a newspaper and sent to libraries, local governments and authorities. This meant that, to engage with the proposal, a citizen would need to be literate and regularly visit such a building in order to submit a response. The proposal only gained 13 responses (Wilson & Perret, 2009).

The current state of engagement in the Australian context

Australian governments at all levels – local, state/territory and federal – have increasingly shown an interest in, and afforded greater priority to, engagement over the past decade. At the federal level, in 2016, Australia's first Open Government National Action Plan was released, with a core commitment to strengthening and improving public participation and engagement (Department of the Prime Minister and Cabinet, 2018). Prior to this, principles relating specifically to consultation requirements were written into the guidelines for completing a Regulation Impact Statement – a necessary step for all Cabinet submissions or decisions in government likely to have a regulatory impact on industry or individuals (Office of Best Practice Regulation, 2017).

These commitments demonstrate an important positive trajectory, even if the numbers don't yet show that the federal government is achieving everything it might in regards to engagement. In fact, measures of how well, or even how much, engagement is being done remain elusive, making it particularly difficult to quantify the current state of engagement.

Another recent initiative to improve stakeholder engagement was the BRII grant, funded by two federal government departments. As described in the introduction to this book, the grant challenged respondents to develop a product that digitally enables community codesign and consultation in policy and program design, in a way that is better, broader and more cost-effective. Collabforge was confident that government didn't need another piece of software to 'do' engagement – there are already so many great applications out there. Instead, we suspected that there was a capability issue that needed to be addressed.

Most training on engagement is done on the job, and it is often just based on what was done last time. We suspected that with a few simple tools, we could build capability, which would help make engagement more consistently practised and get better outcomes for both public servants and stakeholders. We won funding to produce a feasibility study on our recommendation – Scaffle. As a first step, we took a long look at engagement in Australia, well beyond just collaboration. During our desktop research, we read over 80 reports and research papers, compiling our findings to produce a meaningful picture of trends.

Our desktop research was likely to be subject to a number of biases, most critically that the engagements visible online and the reporting on engagement activities tended to be of a larger size than the norm, and as a result were likely to demonstrate a broader range of engagement techniques. That being the case, we supplemented this work with interviews. We spoke with over 30 public servants across 15 departments, at varying levels of government. We used these interviews to test if our desktop research findings reflected the experiences of those working in government.

What we found

For a snapshot of our review of documented consultations/engagements, see Figure 2 overleaf.

We found that, across the Australian federal and state/territory governments, engagement is not well documented. It was interesting to us that no figures were available on how many consultations occur annually across the Australian Public Service (APS), or even within specific departments.

Few departments had teams devoted to assisting with stakeholder engagement design and practice. Where they did, these teams were very busy, and were seldom actually responsible for either delivering or reporting on consultation. This remained in the hands of policy or program officers, typically individuals who did not have specialised training in engagement techniques or practice.

The interviews confirmed our suspicions that the desktop research had only scratched the surface: there were many more consultations going on, almost constantly, and it was very common for these to run in the space of only a few weeks, with no budget to speak of. In talking to public servants, we were honestly surprised at how integral yet under-supported engagement seemed to be.

Almost all of the people we spoke to felt that engagement was a fundamental part of their role:

> 'Consultation is our bread and butter.'

> 'We don't make any significant decisions without consulting.'

> 'It's the majority of what we spend our time doing.'

Figure 2: A summary of our research and findings

Breakdown of the documented consultations/engagements we reviewed:

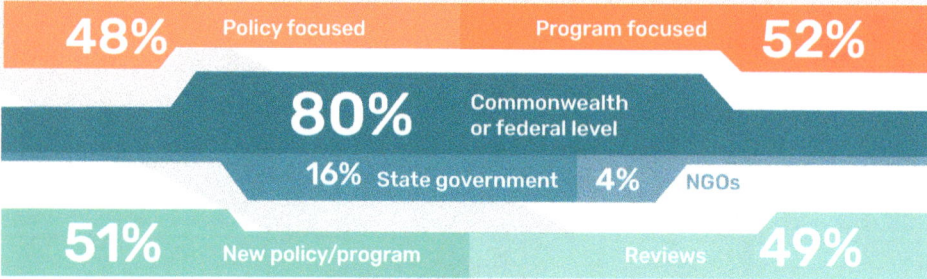

48% Policy focused	Program focused 52%

80% Commonwealth or federal level	

16% State government	4% NGOs

51% New policy/program	Reviews 49%

Average length of engagements

Major policy	3.5 months
New programs	3 months
Program reviews & small–med policies	1–2 months
Average length of engagement period (all)	63 days

In contrast our interviews suggested that many engagements are only

2–4 WEEKS

Level of involvement of all engagement techniques used

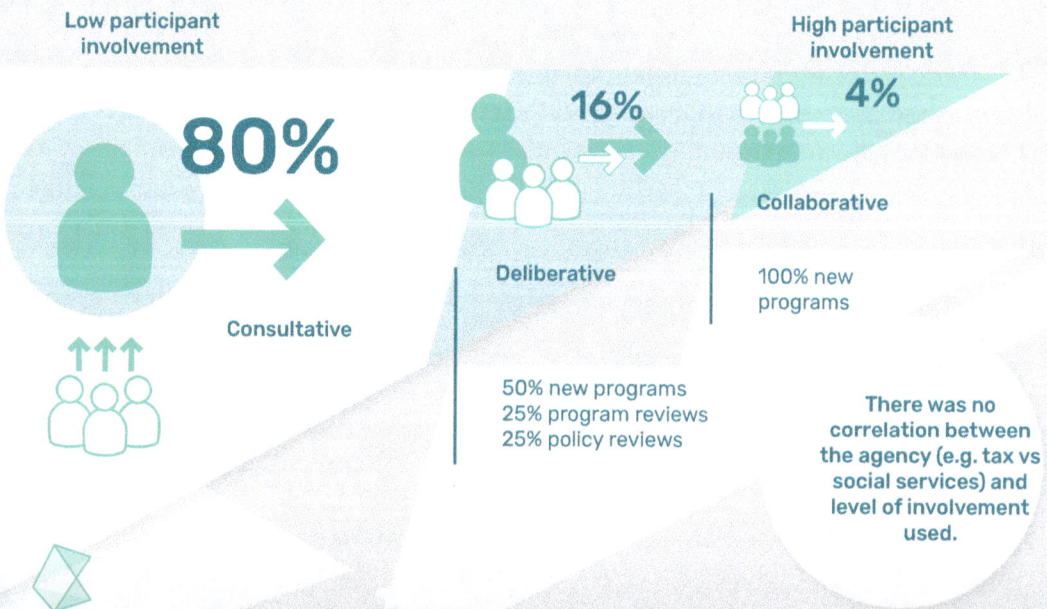

Low participant involvement

80%

Consultative

16%

Deliberative

50% new programs
25% program reviews
25% policy reviews

High participant involvement

4%

Collaborative

100% new programs

There was no correlation between the agency (e.g. tax vs social services) and level of involvement used.

Mix of techniques used to involve participants

Breakdown of write-in techniques

58% Formal response

Over ½ of the projects reviewed only used write-in based methods to engage participants

56% Write-in only

35% Survey

7% Idea proposal

Breakdown of in-person techniques

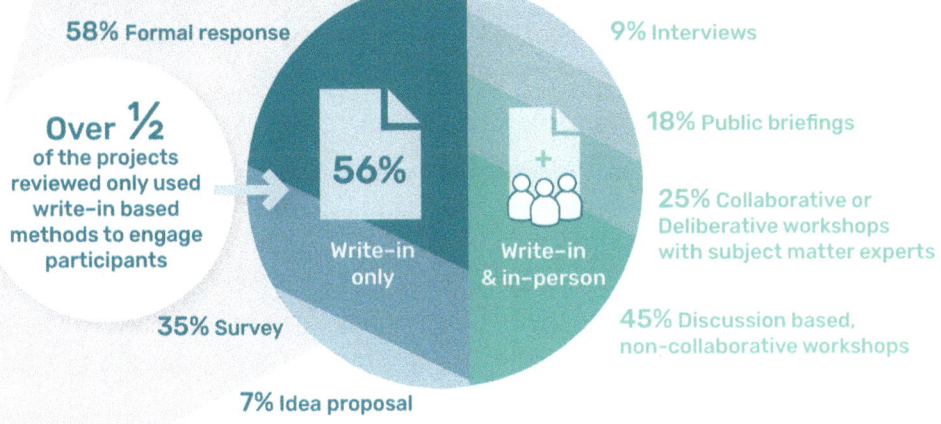

9% Interviews

18% Public briefings

25% Collaborative or Deliberative workshops with subject matter experts

Write-in & in-person

45% Discussion based, non-collaborative workshops

Engagement outputs

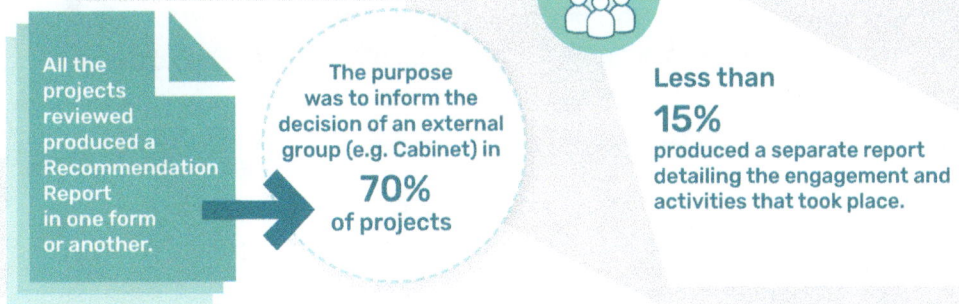

All the projects reviewed produced a Recommendation Report in one form or another.

The purpose was to inform the decision of an external group (e.g. Cabinet) in 70% of projects

Less than 15% produced a separate report detailing the engagement and activities that took place.

¾ of the projects had multiple rounds of engagement, publishing different documents at each stage.

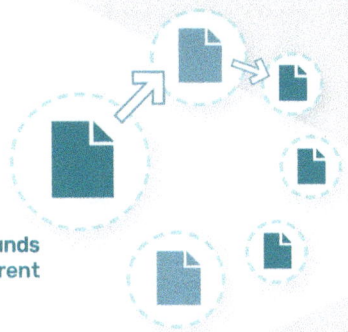

But, by contrast, most felt that there wasn't much investment in capability or engagement practices:

> 'We are not good at consultation because we don't know how to do it. I don't even know what the public tools are … And that's coming from a policy branch.'

> '[We need to remove] some of those barriers that make people go, "Oh, consultation, that's a bit of an effort, too hard".'

> 'Mostly we'll just look around for what we did last time.'

> 'When I first started, I heard all the document terms but didn't understand them.'

This capability gap may explain why four in five engagements only ask for feedback on options, rather than inviting suggestions from participants or their collaborative involvement. We also suspect that there is a substantial amount of engagement that goes undocumented because it occurs very early in the planning stages of a project, such as phone conversations or scoping meetings. A lack of time, knowledge and/or perceived risk further compounds the issue of underdone or under-reported engagement.

At the same time, we found that there was great enthusiasm to do better and to involve stakeholders more. This makes us optimistic that, if some of the challenges in planning and reporting can be addressed, the appetite to make bolder choices in engagement design will grow naturally over time.

Achieving good engagement

Engagement is not something that is extensively covered in the training of policy-makers and public servants, particularly in relation to planning for engagement as a supporting and parallel process to policy and service development. Relationship management, however, is deeply embedded. This means that many policy officers have a natural ability to manage and run engagements with a little bit of support. In order to engage stakeholders, including the public, in ways that feel transparent and fair, we need to address the gap in capability that exists in engagement within the public service. But it should be done in a way that extends and gently improves current practice, rather than creating extra work for already stretched public servants.

There are some embedded ways of thinking that are holding back engagement. In order to get to 'good' engagement, we need to address these. Specifically, we need to acknowledge that:

» engagement shouldn't be thought of as a one-off activity

» the concept of a policy or service delivery cycle can be used to make better engagement choices

» understanding the outcomes you need to achieve can improve your planning

» getting stakeholders involved early, even in the planning stages, will get the best results

» collaboration isn't scary once you know when to plan for it

» better documentation of engagement outcomes will improve public perception.

Engagement isn't a once-and-done activity

While stakeholder engagement is usually described in terms of an activity/ies done at a single point in time, in practice it often occurs in rounds during project stages. For example, the first round of engagement may occur in relation to an issues paper as part of research to determine a policy focus. A second round might be in relation to the drafted policy options. It seems sensible, then, to plan for these rounds of engagement collectively. But this simple concept is almost entirely missing from the existing literature on stakeholder engagement and consultation planning.

There are many handbooks and toolkits for running stakeholder engagement activities. Many focus on specific aspects of these activities – such as asking better questions, or evaluation – and are very useful in that respect. But none really help you to understand how to plan engagement as a parallel process to policy or service delivery and implementation. In order to make it easier to achieve better engagement results, the way we think about and plan for engagement needs to change significantly. Rather than seeing engagement as something outside of the policy or service design project, we must instead see it as an integrated and influential parallel stream of activity.

'Rounds' of engagement are typically marked by the release of documents. This demonstrates the strong connection with a framework commonly known as the policy cycle. We understand that there are tensions in modelling the process of policy (or service delivery) design so simplistically.

However, the marking of a phase as commencing/finishing with the release of a document gives the appearance of a sequential and rational process to external parties. Despite the fact that it may not be a perfect representation, we have found it helpful in framing and planning for engagement.

Figures 3 and 4 show our interpretation of a policy cycle and a service delivery cycle, respectively, with documents linked to each stage. As these documents are developed, they are used as a focus for engagement, enabling input and feedback to finalise the subsequent document. The cycles and the concept of rounds are fundamental to how we suggest engagement is planned – the Scaffle method.

Figure 3: The policy cycle

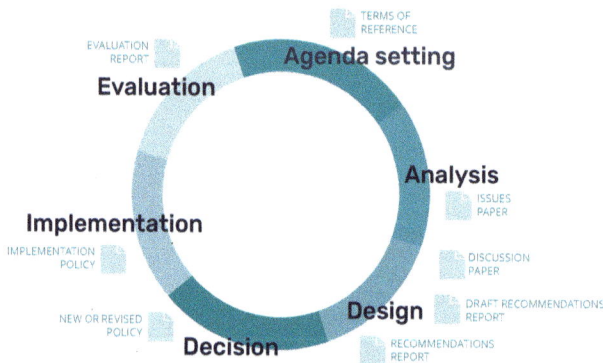

TERMS OF REFERENCE
EVALUATION REPORT
Evaluation
Agenda setting
Analysis
ISSUES PAPER
Implementation
DISCUSSION PAPER
IMPLEMENTATION POLICY
DRAFT RECOMMENDATIONS REPORT
NEW OR REVISED POLICY
Design
Decision
RECOMMENDATIONS REPORT

Source: Adapted from Organisation for Economic Co-operation and Development (2003), p. 34

Figure 4: The service delivery cycle

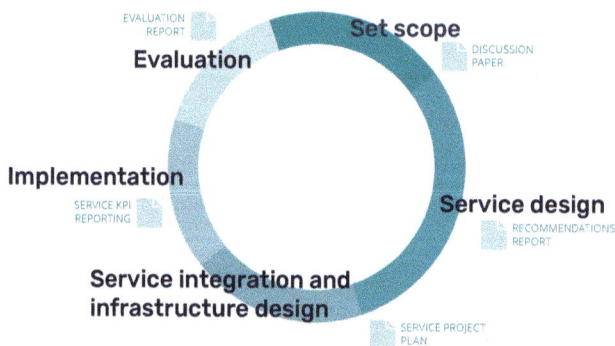

EVALUATION REPORT
Evaluation
Set scope
DISCUSSION PAPER
Implementation
Service design
SERVICE KPI REPORTING
RECOMMENDATIONS REPORT
Service integration and infrastructure design
SERVICE PROJECT PLAN

Sources: Adapted from Department of Finance (2006, 2010)

Small projects may only have one or two stages that incorporate rounds of engagement. Larger projects may expand this model by including additional rounds of engagement in cycle stages; for example, breaking 'Analysis' into 'Research', 'Analysis' and 'Ideation'.

Connecting the cycle model and engagement

To plan engagement in a way that accounts for integration with your policy or service delivery cycle requires understanding what phases and documents you expect to produce in your main project. If you have this mapped out, great; otherwise, the cycle models provide a helpful, if generic, starting point.

Understanding how to plan for engagement as a series of rounds, which structure the activities, seems obvious once explained. It breaks down like this:

» *Engagement plan*: a document that specifies all the details of the engagement rounds and associated activities that will occur at different stages of the policy or service design cycle.

» *Engagement round*: a series of related activities that contribute to the outcomes or outputs of a stage of the policy or service design cycle; for example, finalising a discussion paper during the research stage. You may have more than one round within a stage of the cycle, but each round will have a clear outcome and output to which its activities relate.

» *Engagement activities or techniques*: the single-point methods of interaction with stakeholders that occur within, and contribute to, a particular engagement round.

These elements should not be conflated or confused, as each must be understood and planned for separately. In making the distinctions clear, we have found the analogy of a dinner party to be a helpful one (see Figure 5 overleaf).

Figure 5: A dinner party plan

	Plan	Course	Dish
Outcome: My friends, who don't know each other, become friends	Pre-drinks & nibbles First course Second course Dessert Coffee and games	First course dishes: » Wine (white) » Beer (belgian) » Juice » Water » Falafel croquettes (for vegetarians) » Grilled fish bites (gluten free) Course outcome: Appetites whetted, conversation flowing	Grilled fish bites ingredients: » Fish » Oil » Salt & pepper Attributes (contribute to outcome): Light, easy to eat while talking

A dinner party can have multiple courses involving many dishes that each need to be considered separately – such as what will be needed to cook the fish – but also as a cohesive whole. You might not think of a dinner party as having an 'outcome', especially at the level of the courses. But whether by the intention of an experienced entertainer or the intuition of a good host, each course and dish contributes to how your night goes. For example, do you want to have a perfunctory dinner as a polite nod to in-laws you want out the door by 8.30 p.m.? Or is it to be a lavish affair to cement new friendships? Depending on which it is, you'd naturally adjust the number of courses and the effort you put into cooking accordingly. This is much the same as selecting the rounds and activities in an engagement plan.

Figure 6 gives an example of how this translates into engagement planning.

The 'nested' nature of engagement planning is why it can feel overwhelming or complicated. Having a logic and language to break down the planning for each component as a piece of the whole makes engagement design much simpler and more manageable. If you have years of experience in engagement planning, you might recognise this logic in the methods you have developed for yourself.

Figure 6: An engagement plan

	Plan	Round	Activity
Outcome:	Initial discussion	Agenda setting engagement activities:	Codesign workshop stakeholders:
New policy is delivered and well received	Agenda setting & research	» Internal discussions	» Policy experts
		» Meetings with other department stakeholders	» Subject matter experts
	Analysis		» Industry reps
		» Phone calls to key stakeholders	Output (contributing to outcomes):
	Development	» Codesign workshop	Draft plan and key issues
	Implementation	Outcome:	
	Monitoring & evaluation	Finalised engagement plan ready for publishing & implementation	

Much like the dinner party example, the attributes or output that you want from each activity will vary depending on the round an activity falls in. You wouldn't want to serve an appetiser after dessert, for example. In the same way, care must be taken in selecting engagement activities, to avoid undesired outcomes. You need to adjust your activity selection criteria to match the mode of outcome you are looking to achieve.

Understanding the 'outcomes' of engagement as they relate to policy or service design

Now that we've shown you how outcomes relate to rounds of engagement, we can look at what we mean by 'outcome' and 'outcome modes' more specifically. This in turn can be used to help you select your engagement activities.

'Outcome mode' is a term we use to bundle types of outcomes together. For example, if you are involving stakeholders in the planning of your engagement project, this would be a 'Scoping' mode, as would a risk assessment – these both help determine the process.

To know which mode to use, ask yourself what is the question you are trying to answer by engaging. If you're trying to figure out the issues that need to be addressed, 'Scanning' and 'Exploring' activities will be the most appropriate. If you need to make a decision, be sure to use a 'Confirming' technique.

Figure 7: The Scaffle outcome modes framework

Outcome mode	Examples of desired outcomes
Scoping 'What will our process be?'	» Clarity about what is or isn't possible or permitted in the process » Stakeholder buy-in to the process » Reduced risk of future pitfalls resulting from a bad process
Communicating 'What do we need to say?'	» All stakeholders have the information they need » Impacted parties are aware of what is happening » Improved participation in and quality of engagement activities » All relevant groups have an equal opportunity to contribute » The process is viewed as fair and inclusive (where it's able to be) » Increased compliance with decisions
Scanning 'What do we need to know?'	» Improved shared understanding of the facts of the situation » Organised knowledge and data that can be used in other parts of the process » Assurance that all relevant groups and issues are being considered » Improved systems view
Exploring 'What might be possible?' 'What is feasible?'	» A broad range of possible options » Detail of particular options: how they work or might work in this context » Comparative evaluation of options » Some understanding of measures that should be considered in prioritising steps » Insight into stakeholder needs and preferences » Insight into possible delivery mechanisms (where relevant)
Prioritising 'What are the best options?'	» Organised sets of options » Understanding which options are preferred by which groups » Comparative evaluation of different options » Surfacing tensions generated by differing stakeholder priorities
Confirming 'What will we recommend?' 'What should we do?'	» Decision-making process articulated » Resolution of tensions – at least to the point of increased acceptance of the steps being taken » Option selected / recommendations made » Outcomes of formal decision made clear

Figure 7 shows our outcome modes framework – the modes, questions, and examples of typical outcomes you might be seeking to achieve in relation to your policy or service design.

Unlike the policy cycle, the outcome modes framework is not intended to be linear. Outcome modes are simply meant to help you select engagement activities for each engagement round.

We have found that there are standard patterns regarding how outcome modes relate to the policy and service delivery cycles. Figures 8 and 9 show how they may flow across typical cycles.

Figure 8: Typical outcome modes of a policy based engagement plan

Engagement plan	
Engagement round	» **Outcome mode**
Agenda setting & research	» Scoping
Analysis	» Scanning
	» Exploring
	» Prioritising
Design	» Prioritising
	» Confirming
	» Communicating
Decision	» Confirming
	» Communicating
Implementation	» Scoping
	» Communicating
Monitoring & evaluation	» Scanning

Figure 9: Typical outcome modes of a service delivery engagement plan

Engagement plan	
Engagement round »	Outcome mode
Set scope	» Scoping
Service design	» Scanning
	» Exploring
	» Prioritising
	» Confirming
Service integration and infrastructure design	» Exploring
	» Prioritising
	» Confirming
	» Communicating
Implementation	» Communicating
Evaluation	» Scoping
	» Communicating

Prioritising engagement in the planning stages

The best opportunity for real collaboration and influence arises in the earliest stages of planning a project. You may not be able to give or promise much influence to a group regarding what the outcomes will be, or how a decision will be made, but that group can have a big impact through helping you understand who to talk to, where to find information, and what are the most important issues that you need to be aware of.

Too often, planning for a project is done in isolation. If a committee or panel has not been allocated to run a project, it may be planned entirely without external input. This misses a huge opportunity, as it is the number-one way to improve outcomes. It's an uncomfortable spot for public servants to be in: asking for input on a plan at the agenda-setting stage, before you've even finalised your problem definition or tabled the issues at hand. However, this is the best time to bring in your subject-matter experts for some real collaboration.

Codesign in the agenda-setting and planning stages of your project can significantly influence the issues tabled for resolution, and the recommendations that are ultimately developed and approved. Working groups and committees naturally perform this function in large engagements, checking that the right stakeholders are approached and that the research design is adequate and unbiased. The same principle can be used in a small, time-pressured project through a short codesign session in person or digitally.

Even if you feel that the project has been planned and the opportunity to collaborate on that plan has been missed, question this premise. Could you email an outline of your engagement plan to a colleague with specialist knowledge for their input? Could you check in with an industry expert on your proposed stakeholder list? Input on your engagement plan not only helps you identify your blind spots, it is also a great thing to report on. Building the plan through engagement will ensure that you can justify why you selected your stakeholders and activities when you report on those activities later on.

Later, we go into more detail on how you can use engagement in your planning, in the section 'Why it's best to engage from the outset' (see page 68).

Collaboration isn't scary once you know when to plan for it

Consultative modes of involvement are often used because they feel less risky than deliberative, or especially collaborative, modes. This is usually because real collaboration means you are not in control of the output. Sometimes this is beneficial – when it leads to an idea or result that you wouldn't have arrived at by inviting the collaboration, for example. However, sometimes it is not desirable, such as when the group designs a solution that goes against what a minister has announced or planned. Informative and consultative modes are more appropriate at the points in your process where you need control but still want validation or an understanding of the concerns of stakeholders. When you genuinely want input that could inform and change your solution, opt for collaborative or deliberative modes. If you aren't sure which is the case for you, understanding where you are at in your process can be a helpful indicator. Much in the same way that all types of outcomes are unlikely to be relevant to a particular round, the typical mode of involvement also changes over the course of an engagement project.

Timing modes of involvement differently for the policy and service delivery cycles

Policy design starts with a challenge to solve, rather than a predetermined 'how'. Ideally, there are no preconceived 'solutions'. Rather, the process starts with thorough research in order to determine the issues and to form solutions. This means that, at the outset, stakeholders have a significant ability to influence the final policy outcome by unearthing critical research and raising key issues. As a solution forms, though, they have less and less ability to influence the outcomes, able only to raise concerns with the given solution.

Service delivery or program design, by contrast, is typically commenced as a result of a policy or similar decision that has determined the relevant needs and fundamentals. If early engagement is undertaken, this is usually limited to feedback on these fundamentals. The commencement of the implementation design is when the real opportunity for influence presents itself, with all sorts of collaborations often needed to determine the delivery methods. This can continue well into implementation.

Depending on which stage of the cycle you are in, the most appropriate modes of involvement for engagement may change. Figure 10 shows how the use of the mode of involvement may be more or less appropriate throughout a policy or service delivery cycle. There are times when you might want a whole process to be a collaborative, innovative example of engagement potential. But in regular, everyday, hurried engagements, there are opportunities to improve the influence of the participants. It's just about catching them at the right time.

Figure 10: Mapping the mode of involvement to the policy and service cycles

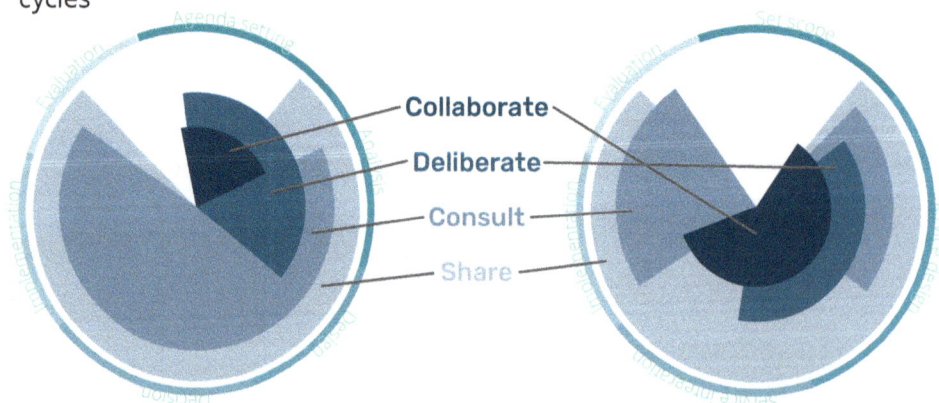

Documentation provides transparency

A lot of engagement is invisible to stakeholders. It can even be invisible to other areas of the same department. In order to improve the perception of engagement, better documentation and reporting is required, to help stakeholders understand how and why decisions have been made.

Once you start planning for engagement in parallel to the policy and service delivery cycles, you'll notice there are opportunities for engagement that you might not have considered. You may also find there are things you are doing that should be documented as engagement but which are not being recorded. In both cases, you can make a better case for your final recommendations and demonstrate a thoroughness to your approach that would otherwise be hard to articulate.

In our experience, stakeholders who give their time to an engagement feel invested in the outcomes and are keen to know what was made of their input. Producing an engagement report can help with this, but the cost in time needs to be managed. This became central to Collabforge's thinking in developing Scaffle. Having the engagement planning and results in one place makes it easy to pull together a report documenting who was engaged, at which points they were engaged or re-engaged, and how the outputs of engagement collectively influenced the decision-makers.

If you're not using the Scaffle application for your project, we suggest you think carefully about how to manage your information throughout the process. Good filing practices can make a world of difference when pulling reports together or responding to any questions that arise during or after your project.

Regardless, it can be very worthwhile producing a report that provides feedback to stakeholders. It demonstrates that you value their contributions. And the transparency of this quietens the voices of those opposed to the outcomes, as they at least feel they have been heard, even if their preferences weren't selected.

Supporting engagement planning

Possibly the most important organisational or systemic change for improving the capability of public servants in planning and delivering stronger engagement is to provide better access to information. The efficient provision of information streamlines any planning, reducing the burden for public servants; specifically:

» information on engagement techniques

» better information on suppliers and pricing

» recommendations on relevant new technologies.

Information on possible engagement techniques

Often, we don't try something new simply because we don't know what options we have. For example, there are literally hundreds of ways in which to engage stakeholders, but most people can only name a handful of them. Many of the techniques are variations on a theme but for a specific situation, such as when there is low trust, or conflict. That being the case, an easy-to-use reference for discovering and learning about techniques would be a low-cost way of improving engagement planning.

We have compiled a number of techniques in this book (see Part Four; page 97). And we have written about them specifically in the context of a public servant using them to develop a policy or service. This quick-reference guide offers a simple and easy way of immediately expanding your engagement vocabulary. We hope it is a handy starting point for you as you plan for better engagement.

Our reference guide is set to become even more useful as we expand it online through the Scaffle application, with the help of other experts. Visit the Scaffle website (http://scaffle.com.au/engage) to deepen your understanding of engagement techniques.

Better information about suppliers and pricing

Here are some scenarios you might be familiar with.

Marli has been tasked with planning an engagement project. She would like to use an engagement technique that has a codesign aspect, but she doesn't feel confident *managing her stakeholders through the process herself. Marli needs to get the plan back to her manager today and needs to figure out how much budget she should allow for. She makes a few calls internally and gets estimates ranging from $15K to $50K. She knows that she might be able to get approval if it's under $20K, but not if it's more. She is given a lead on a potential provider, but they don't return her call. In order to streamline her planning and hit her deadline, she changes the technique to one she is more familiar with – one that she knows won't have an external cost.*

For another project, Marli chooses to go to tender because she needs to get specific quotes in order to budget for a requested activity. She is expecting the quotes to be in the range of $20K to $50K, but all four responses have budgets in excess of $100K. Marli responds to each that the work is not proceeding and alters her plan to exclude the activity.

We think it's best if planners can access information on potential costs that allows them to make informed planning choices, even if these are not 100% precise or based on broad ranges. This allows for better budgeting and avoids tendering processes that waste everyone's time when expectations are misaligned.

While this issue is not easy to solve in this book, we suggest that procurement systems need to evolve to do a better job of helping you in the future. We are attempting to address this in the Scaffle digital application through an industry-managed database that includes better pricing indicators from suppliers. We think this information is critical in allowing you to be more creative and strategic in your planning processes.

Better data processing and the evolving role of technology

We are very fortunate to live in a time when technology is evolving at unprecedented speeds. Developing AI technologies mean that you can analyse information in ways not previously possible. There are two key ways in which this can help you in engagement. The first is general research to understand a stakeholder group, and the second is the analysis of large amounts of quantitative and qualitative data.

At the outset of your project, you may be seeking a general quantitative analysis of how your public stakeholders feel about a subject. There are a number of systems out there that can search across multiple social media and news channels to help you understand what your stakeholders are sharing, and what this implies about their interest in your subject. This can save you considerable money over traditional market research, and may provide some interesting insights (while being aware of their limitations and bias; for example, only a sub-set of your group may discuss topics online).

We also understand that not knowing how to process all the information received can be a barrier to using some engagement methods, such as roundtables or unconferences. Processing feedback can become a mammoth undertaking, especially if thousands of responses are received. If this task falls entirely to one person, it can easily overwhelm them, leading to summaries that aren't as comprehensive as they could be, and to key feedback being missed. In our experience, summarising even a hundred responses quickly becomes a monotonous and difficult task. This gets worse if the person doing the analysis doesn't have a strong grasp of data analysis processes or a good research framework.

Our sister company in the BRII grant program, Converlens, is working on AI technology that can help make sense of your qualitative data for you with a significant reduction in effort (or potentially cost, as there are agencies that offer a human-based version of this service). The technology is still in the testing stages, but we are excited to see if this will make shorter work of the grind of qualitative analysis, freeing you up to scan responses for interesting insights. This could turn many activities that produce complex information which goes unused, into ones that uncover meaningful data for better policy and service outcomes.

2 The Scaffle method for engagement planning

The Scaffle method is our process for creating a holistic engagement plan. We will now walk you through the steps, making you more confident in selecting engagement activities and knowing how each will contribute to your policy or service design project. We think of this as the framing – the scaffolding – that will support your project outcomes.

This part of the book covers:

» where to start in building your plan outline – your 'scaffold'

» how to choose and sequence engagement activities

» how to plan and run an engagement activity

» why you should engage as early as the planning stage, if possible.

Building your scaffold

This process works whether you are running a policy or service delivery–based project. For the sake of simplicity – so we don't have to say 'policy or service delivery' all the time – from this point on we'll assume that you're running a policy-based project. If this isn't the case, the same principles regarding how to determine your rounds and engagement activities still apply; you'll simply name your rounds differently (see Figures 3 and 4 on for detail on how the two cycles typically differ; page 24). As terminology is one of those things that can differ considerably, even between departments, you may find that you would naturally use different language to ours even if you were running a policy-based engagement project. Regardless, it is the process described here that is important. The semantics should be determined by your needs and organisational culture.

Your 'scaffold' is your engagement plan outline. It can be pulled together quickly, but it should have enough depth to enable you to rapidly fill in the details and flesh out a final engagement plan. The steps involved are as follows:

1. Determine the rounds you'll need.
2. Work out the timing of your rounds.
3. Assign outcomes to your rounds.

This outline will provide the information you need to move on to selecting and planning your engagement activities in the next section: 'Choosing and sequencing engagement activities' (see page 48).

Identifying your rounds of engagement

Identifying the rounds of engagement your project will likely go through is the first step in developing your engagement plan. You should begin by considering the information you've been provided with, such as the timing, documents required, if you have a budget, and so on. These are your key requirements or limitations, so your plan will need to reflect them. You might have an end date, or delivery dates for specific documents. There might also be key stakeholders who you have been asked to involve. If you have quite a few specifications, or they're in different source documents such as emails or meeting notes, take a minute to find them. Jotting them down under the following headings is a useful way to start structuring your thinking:

- » key dates
- » key outputs (documents or other artefacts you've been asked to develop)
- » key stakeholders
- » other requirements.

Starting your project from scratch is ideal, but this isn't always possible. Fortunately, the Scaffle method is beneficial even if you aren't starting with a blank page. So whether you've inherited a project that is already underway, or you're only just beginning to think about engagement after identifying the relevant issues, it's not too late. Start by writing down key information about any work that has already been completed. Tracking what the project has accomplished will help you spot gaps and will be useful for selecting your engagement activities.

After identifying the key information, and whether or not any work has already been completed, you will end up with something like this:

KEY DATES	KEY OUTPUTS	KEY STAKEHOLDERS	OTHER REQUIREMENTS
» Final recommendations doc required 30 Oct » Issues paper requested completed 30 June (complete: 20 June) » New work to commence 1 July	» Issues paper » Final recommendations doc	» Minister's office » Special ed. peak body » Parents	» Need to send all drafts to Secretary prior to release » No budget given; likely to manage internally if possible

This hypothetical example, which we'll continue to develop throughout this section, tells us a few things. We know that we'll probably undertake engagement at least twice, and we know that any engagement on the issues paper has to end before 30 June, and engagement on the final recommendations has to end before 30 October:

Engagement 1 → Issues paper → Engagement 2 → Final recommendations doc

Next, we also know that everything up until the issues paper has already been completed, but we now need to determine what to do with the 17 weeks up until 30 October.

We want to map out possible rounds of engagement based on this information (refer back to the 'Engagement isn't a once-and-done activity' section for more detail on the concept of rounds; page 23). Figure 11 (see overleaf) provides a reference table for the policy cycle that explains how this translates into:

- » rounds of engagement (one or more engagement activities designed to help you complete a single task/outcome)
- » effort (the percentage of available time you might spend on rounds)
- » outputs (the physical documents you might create through the process)
- » outcomes (what you are trying to achieve at each stage).

Figure 11: Policy cycle reference table

Cycle stage	Policy purpose	Effort	Rounds/sub-rounds
1. Agenda setting	Determine goals and scope of project. Articulate the need and problem to be addressed, and who is affected.	25%	» Agenda setting » Scope confirmation » Problem confirmation » Stakeholder identification » Risk identification
2. Analysis	Conduct research into facts and opinion, undertake exploratory thinking, and ideation.	35%	» Research » Analysis » Ideation » Solution identification
3. Design	Evaluation, prioritisation and selection of solution options. Arrive at a preferred solution, explicitly expressed and ready for decision-making and implementation.	30%	» Solution prioritisation » Design / draft options » Evaluate options » Select preferred options » Confirm preferred options » Draft final policy/service plan » Finalise policy/service plan
4. Decision	Provide official confirmation of the preferred solution.	10%	» Decision/vote
5. Implementation	Make the chosen solution a reality, May include planning for implementation, as well as ongoing monitoring, feedback and adaptation.		» Plan for implementation » Implementation » Measurement during implementation
6. Evaluation	Determine the impact of the implemented solution, in order to inform future activities.		» Plan for evaluation » Evaluation & review

Engagement outcomes	Example outputs
Mode: Scoping Engagement during this round will set the tone for the whole project, and will reduce risk and improve outcomes by delivering key insights and stakeholder alignment early.	» Terms of reference » Confirmed engagement plan
Modes: Scanning, Exploring, Prioritising Engagement during this round will improve the understanding of the problem and expand the pool of potential solutions.	» Issues paper or discussion paper, to confirm the problem space » Discussion paper or options paper, to prioritise probable solutions
Modes: Prioritising, Confirming, Communicating Engagement during this round will increase stakeholder trust and buy-in to the chosen solution, and improve the quality of the policy documents themselves.	» Draft recommendations report, to confirm solution details » Final recommendations report, to ensure solution is ready for decision–makers
Modes: Confirming, Communicating Engagement during this round is primarily about communicating the decision-making process, and the rationale for and consequences of the decision that was made.	» Parliamentary proceedings » Meeting minutes » Engagement report » Policy
Modes: Scoping, Confirming, Communicating Engagement during this round can improve the likelihood that policy intent will be successfully translated, reduce implementation risks by increasing the amount of information available, improve voluntary compliance, and reduce friction when changes and adaptations need to be made.	» Implementation strategy or plan, to determine how the policy or service will be delivered or enforced » Implementation data
Mode: Scanning Engagement during this round can help ensure that what is being measured is of value to stakeholders, increase participation in measurement activities, and increase trust in the results of the evaluation.	» Evaluation report, to assess how well the policy or service delivered is addressing the problem space

Figure 11 is an imperfect illustration of the relationship between these elements. We've named the elements according to our usage, but your organisation probably has its own, more specific language. Still, this is a starting point for locating yourself in the policy cycle, and identifying the right rounds of engagement for you.

Looking at the figure, we can see that 'Agenda setting' has already been completed for our project and we are currently in the 'Analysis' cycle stage. We know this because we have a completed issues paper. To translate this into an engagement plan, we can initially map this through numbering, as shown below, to name our engagement rounds, including what has already been done. Feel free to rename or add rounds according to what makes the most sense for your project – these principles are about structuring, not semantics.

1. Agenda setting (complete)
2. Research to identify options (complete)
3. Define and prioritise solutions (can start now)
4. Draft recommendations report
5. Confirm final recommendations (ends 30 Oct)
6. Implement solution (proposed to commence 1 Jan)
7. Measure and review

It's helpful to include stages that have been completed to ensure, in turn, completeness in reporting. If you're going to report on the engagement conducted in order to produce a policy or service, you'll need to know what happened and who has been engaged throughout the *whole* process.

Scenario: Identifying rounds using outputs

Documents, as a physical output of a round, can be a helpful way of identifying where rounds occur, or where they can be added or split. Generally, all the engagement of a round can be seen as helping develop the document output for the round. For example, research to help define or analyse the problem space will provide the input needed to produce an issues paper.

In some cases, you may be asked to produce specific documents. This is a sign that you will need a certain type of round in order to produce that document. For example, a discussion paper is usually the result of a round that creates and prioritises solutions.

If you have more than one document output allocated to a round, this could mean you are trying to do too many things in that round and you need to break it down, as shown in the following example:

1. Agenda setting:
   a. Output: Approved project plan
2. Problem identification:
   a. Output: Issues paper
3. Prioritising solutions:
   a. Output: Options paper
   b. Output: Draft recommendations *(two outputs here may indicate that this round should be split into two rounds: one to identify options and a second to confirm or prioritise them)*
4. Implementation planning:
   a. Output: Implementation plan
5. Evaluation:
   a. Output: Evaluation report

Assigning timing to rounds

Timing rounds is a bit of a chicken-and-egg game. You need to know how much time you have in each round to pick the right engagement activities, but in some cases you'll want to know how much time you need to plan and run an engagement activity in order to plan your rounds. There isn't a single right way – your approach should be determined by your needs and risks rather than by a single formula.

Percentages are a useful starting point when thinking about timing. We would recommend allowing the longest time (the greatest percentage) to the rounds that have less clarity and require more thinking. This is because in these rounds it is hard to take short cuts and still get a good outcome. They can also be the rounds that throw up the biggest curve balls, like identifying a whole stakeholder group you've missed, or risks you haven't anticipated that may cost you extra time.

The use of percentages also allows you to quickly map time based on the type of work that will be done in the round, without considering the practicalities. This can help you highlight time-based risks when you convert the percentages into actual weeks.

For instance, in our hypothetical example, we need to plan for the following rounds (we'll ignore completed rounds for now):

3. Define and prioritise solutions (can start now)
4. Draft recommendations report
5. Confirm final recommendations (ends 30 Oct)
6. Implement solution (proposed to commence 1 Jan)
7. Measure and review

'Define and prioritise solutions' seems to be the round with the greatest potential for ambiguity. Once we have a preferred solution, it should be fairly straightforward to draft a recommendations paper, even if it brings up a few more problems to solve. Resolving the last few objections into a final report is likely to be known territory. In this example, we don't actually have responsibility for creating the implementation plan, so we don't need to allocate time to that round. The last two rounds should be planned for and scheduled but don't need a time percentage allocation. So our time planning might look something like this:

3. Define and prioritise solutions: 50% (starts 1 July)
4. Draft recommendations report: 30%
5. Confirm final recommendations: 20% (ends 30 Oct)
6. Implement solution (proposed to commence 1 Jan)
7. Measure and review (schedule 12 months from 1 Jan)

Since we have 17 weeks between commencement and 30 October, we can allocate weeks into the following first-draft plan:

3. Define and prioritise solutions: 8 weeks, 1 July – 26 Aug (50%)
4. Draft recommendations report: 5 weeks, 27 Aug – 30 Sept (30%)
5. Confirm final recommendations: 4 weeks, 1–28 Oct (20%)
6. Implement solution (proposed to commence 1 Jan)
7. Measure and review (schedule 12 months from 1 Jan)

Looking at our original notes, we also need to allow for documents for engagement to be reviewed and approved by the Secretary. This will probably take a week at the end of each round. We also want to make sure our weeks start on a Monday. If we allow a week for writing output documents too, then our engagement rounds might shift slightly:

3. Define and prioritise solutions:

   a. Engagement: 6 weeks, 1 July – 12 Aug (50%)

   b. Draft and get approval for options paper: 2 weeks, 13–26 Aug

4. Draft recommendations report:

   a. Engagement: 3 weeks, 27 Aug – 16 Sept (30%)

   b. Draft and get approval for recommendations paper: 2 weeks, 17–30 Sept

5. Confirm final recommendations:

   a. Engagement: 2 weeks, 1–14 Oct (20%)

   b. Draft and get approval for final recommendations paper: 2 weeks, 15–28 Oct

6. Implement solution (proposed to commence 1 Jan)

7. Measure and review (schedule 12 months from 1 Jan)

This is still a little optimistic time-wise, but it gives us a starting point for planning engagement activities. First, though, there is one more step to do: review these rounds using the outcome modes framework.

Scenario: Identifying rounds using time

Don't have much information about document outputs but have clear deadlines? You can use your deadlines to create rounds. In order to determine how many rounds you can complete, start with your end date and work backwards. In an ideal situation, one where you have plenty of time (don't laugh, it might happen), or for a high-profile or high-risk project, you'd want to ensure you have at least the rounds discussed in Figure 11. It's best to allow more time for the earlier stages so that you can do adequate stakeholder analysis and research, or work out solutions over the prioritisation or confirmation stages.

1. Agenda setting and research (25%)

2. Research and identify options (35%)

3. Test and improve solution (30%)

4. Determine implementation plan (10%)

5. Measure and review (ideally scheduled but not included in time allocation)

The heavier weighting on earlier rounds may initially seem a little counterintuitive. If you missed it, go back and read the 'Prioritising engagement in the planning stages' section in Part One (see page 30).

If you only have a few weeks, there might not be enough time to go through many rounds. Or for policy reviews that are a matter of function, such as annually scheduled reviews, some rounds may not be applicable. In such cases, eliminate or merge rounds. You can use the output method to help you check this.

1. Agenda setting and planning (10% – pretty much predetermined by what we did last year, 2 days):

    a. Output: Documentation of proposed review process

2. ~~Research and identify options (40%)~~ *(Will let this be determined by responses in round 3)*

3. Evaluate implementation of current policy (60%, 2 weeks)

4. Confirm any updates (30%, 1 week)

5. Review (scheduled but not included in time allocation)

Assigning outcomes to rounds

Understanding what you are trying to achieve – your desired outcome – is critical for the strategic selection of engagement activities. An 'outcome' in this context is the result you need to achieve in order to progress your project with confidence. Outcomes and outcome modes were covered in the section 'Understanding the "outcomes" of engagement as they relate to policy or service delivery' (see page 27).

Within each round, you may have to achieve several things in order to get all the information you need to write your output document. For example, in the agenda-setting round, you may need to achieve the following:

» confirm that all the relevant stakeholders have been considered

» understand the key primary and secondary sources of information

» map and understand the key risks and likely areas of conflict

» get approval for your inclusive and effective engagement plan.

At a high level, the questions you need to ask to get to these outcomes are along the lines of 'What do we need to know?' and 'What should our process be?'. This suggests that they connect to our outcome modes framework by:

» mapping the territory (scanning)

» planning (scoping).

You need to determine the outcomes, and their order if you have more than one, for each round in your plan. Returning to our hypothetical example, we can identify outcome modes and outcomes for each of our rounds as follows:

3. Define and prioritise solutions:

    a. Engagement: 6 weeks, 1 July – 12 Aug (50%)

    b. Outcomes:

        i.   Exploring – develop a range of feasible solutions; get insight into stakeholder perceptions of options

        ii. Prioritising – comparative analysis of solutions; surface any known tensions about the proposed options

    c. Output: Draft and get approval for options paper

4. Draft recommendations report:

    a. Engagement: 3 weeks, 27 Aug – 16 Sept (30%)

    b. Outcomes:

        i.   Communicating – ensure all stakeholders know we have a draft recommendation

        ii. Confirming – surface and resolve tensions; clarify details of the recommendation

    c. Draft and get approval for recommendations paper

5. Confirm final recommendations:

    a. Engagement: 2 weeks, 1–14 Oct (20%)

    b. Outcomes:

        i.   Communicating – ensure all stakeholders know we have a final recommendation; let stakeholders know what will happen next

        ii. Confirming – finalise any last details

        iii. Scanning – gauge likely reactions

    c. Draft and get approval for final recommendations paper

6. Implement solution (proposed to commence 1 Jan)

7. Measure and review (schedule 12 months from 1 Jan)

This engagement plan 'scaffold' gives us all the steps and stages we can consider for our project. We now have all the information we need to start mapping engagement activities to our plan, as we can look for activities to match the outcomes we have identified. You might already be aware of all these details when you are planning. However, laying this logic out quickly and clearly means that you can devote more time to thinking creatively and strategically about your engagement activities.

Choosing and sequencing engagement activities

Did you know that there are probably hundreds of different engagement techniques out there you can use to involve stakeholders? I'm sure you can name a handful, but there are many you might not have heard of that can help in specific scenarios. We differentiate between 'techniques' and 'activities' in this book only in that a technique is the method described/prescribed as the way to deliver an engagement, and an activity is the engagement that you'll actually be designing and running – a version of that technique tailored to your unique purpose and needs. There are 35 techniques outlined for your reference in Part Four of this book (see page 97).

Having even 35 techniques to decide between would be overwhelming if you hadn't already created a neat and clear framework to quickly narrow in on the activities that are relevant to you. Once you use your outcome mode to filter (either in Part Four using the outcome mode quick reference, or by using the online filters in our Scaffle platform), you start to get a more manageable number to assess. Factor in the time required and whether you can run it yourself, or need outside experts, and you'll have an even narrower set.

To help you choose which techniques are right for you, and start tailoring them to your purpose, the following sections outline how to:

» match techniques to the right outcome mode

» factor in involvement modes

» make the most of the time you have available

» sequence activities

» match activities to your risk profile

» plan if you have to 'do it yourself'

» be ready for reporting.

Getting the right outcome

Outcome modes are useful for narrowing down the set of activities, but you'll need to get even more specific when you're choosing activities. Think carefully about what you need to achieve. What will be most useful to you for where you'll be at in your policy/service project? Do you just need to see the trends in what people are thinking, or do you need actual ideas from them? Do you want your thinking checked for gaps? Or should the stakeholders directly create the recommendation and you'll check it? In the simplest terms, how can you use engagement to get an efficient project outcome, while also maximising the chance of a great policy/service outcome for stakeholders?

The engagement techniques detailed in this book have been written to help you quickly understand what kinds of outcomes they can support you with. Some techniques can help you with more than one outcome, so while they are grouped by 'primary' outcome, you should use the table in Figure 12 to cross-reference all the techniques you might consider.

Figure 12: Engagement activities sorted by outcome modes

Scoping	Communicating	Scanning
» Collaborative problem definition	» Advertising	» Bilateral meeting
» Codesign process	» Factsheet	» Citizens' panel
	» Freecall / 1800 numbers	» Collaborative problem definition
	» Information kit	» Community mapping
	» Interactive e-conferencing	» Community or public meeting
	» Media event	» Computer-assisted participation
	» Trade show or exhibition	» Consensus conference
		» Consensus forum
		» Consultative interview
		» Deliberative polling
		» Focus group
		» Issues conference
		» Polling
		» Search conference
		» Survey
		» Unconference

(Figure continues overleaf)

Exploring	Prioritising	Confirming
» Advisory committee, board or council	» Advisory committee, board or council	» Advisory committee, board or council
» Call for submissions	» Call for submissions	» Call for submissions
» Charrette	» Citizens' jury	» Community or public meeting
» Codesign process	» Codesign process	» Computer assisted participation
» Community or public meeting	» Computer-assisted participation	» Constituent assembly
» Consultative interview	» Constituent assembly	» Consultative interview
» Deliberative polling	» Consultative interview	» Delphi process
» Ideas challenge	» Deliberative polling	» Nominal group process
» Issues conference	» Delphi process	» Policy Wiki
» Nominal group process	» Focus group	» Survey
» Roundtable	» Nominal group process	
» Search conference	» Policy Wiki	
» Unconference	» Polling	
	» Roundtable	
	» Search conference	
	» Survey	

Using involvement modes

If your engagement choices are still overwhelming, you might consider what mode of involvement you would like to use (see the 'Understanding modes of involvement' section for more details; "Using involvement modes" on page 50). Collaborative modes can be particularly effective in the early rounds, when you aren't claiming to have all the answers and are open to the input of stakeholders regarding the process.

If there are a few techniques you're considering, it might be helpful to write these down and then group them by involvement mode, to form a clearer picture of your choices. Before you make a decision, consider if the mode of involvement you would *like* to use is realistic for your circumstances. Asking for ideas, for example, is not appropriate if youroutcome is 90% predetermined.

The involvement mode is a good thing to keep in mind when you're inviting stakeholders to an engagement. You can use it to check their expectations and communicate effectively about how you are asking them to be involved.

The table in Figure 13 cross-references techniques against outcome mode and involvement mode.

Figure 13: Engagement activities sorted by involvement modes

Share	Consult	Deliberate	Collaborate
» Advertising	» Bilateral meeting	» Advisory committee, board or council	» Charrette
» Community or public meeting	» Call for submissions	» Charrette	» Citizens' jury
» Factsheet	» Citizens' panel	» Citizens' jury	» Codesign process
» Free call / 1800 numbers	» Community or public meeting	» Codesign process	» Collaborative problem definition
» Information kit	» Computer-assisted participation	» Computer-assisted participation	» Community mapping
» Interactive e-conferencing	» Consensus conference	» Deliberative polling	» Constituent assembly
» Media event	» Consensus forum	» Ideas challenge	» Ideas challenge
» Trade show or exhibition	» Consultative interview	» Issues conference	» Policy Wiki
	» Deliberative polling	» Policy Wiki	» Search conference
	» Delphi process	» Roundtable	
	» Focus group	» Unconference	
	» Issues conference		
	» Nominal group process		
	» Polling		
	» Roundtable		
	» Survey		
	» Unconference		

Timing the activity

Time is often the biggest deciding factor when it comes to running engagement activities. Most of the techniques themselves only take a day or less to actually deliver, but making sure you have enough time to get into everyone's calendars can require weeks of forward planning, especially if you need to get executives or members of the public on board. You may have to get a little creative to fit something into your round. Maybe one of your key stakeholders isn't available for a workshop, but you can get them on the phone for a half-hour interview. Perhaps you can deliver a webinar rather than try to bring together geographically dispersed stakeholders. Or perhaps, upon looking at the timing and options, you can recommend an extension, as it's critical to the outcomes that an activity not be rushed or exclude any stakeholders.

Compressing lead times usually just means a lot more legwork on your part; for example, rather than expecting stakeholders to work to your schedule, you'll need to call them all individually and find a time slot that works for them. Or you may need to go to them, instead of expecting them to come to you. The times we suggest for the activities in Part Four are just a guide – you'll need to adjust these to match your circumstances. And remember that just because something appears to need a longer lead time doesn't mean you can't get it to work with a little elbow grease.

When you're considering lead and delivery times for an activity, also consider the integration time. Some activities, such as a co-written plan, might have the output almost delivered during the activity. But most will require you or your facilitators to do some work to make the outputs meaningful to your project. For example, roundtable events or interviews could leave you with a large number of qualitative notes that will need analysing and categorising.

Sometimes, there are things you can do to reduce this integration work. You could put a staff member at each table at the roundtable event and task them with recording themes, then bring them all together at a workshop to discuss the themes and look for commonalities or any outlying information that might be critical to your process. Reducing the integration work usually requires a little more forward planning – thinking about the types of responses you're expecting or need, designing thoughtful questions, and carefully planning ways of recording. But this up-front work will probably save you a lot of time on integration and is highly worthwhile.

The techniques indexed in Part Four specify both a lead-time and a run-time range to provide a general guide to timing. This is obviously flexible and can be used in combination with the above suggestions to schedule activities that fit into your available time allocation.

Sequencing activities

The order in which you schedule activities can impact the results you get. For example, scheduling a survey might yield statistics that you can't adequately explain. These could then be explored by a focus group to give you the 'why' behind the trends you're seeing, so you avoid making uniformed assumptions. By contrast, having a focus group before a survey can help you figure out the best questions to ask, or help you learn more about the particular language that will connect with your audience. That way, when you run your survey, you will be more confident that the cost is well worth it, as the audience is more likely to understand, and respond better, to the way in which the questions are posed.

If you are planning on running more than one type of engagement activity in your round, consider what types of outputs you're likely to get from each activity. How might this influence, or be influenced by, the outputs of your other activities? Is there a particular sequence for which it would be most beneficial to resolve any possible risks or get a better outcome?

Tuning for risk

We introduced the two main types of high-level risk in the section 'Reducing risk' (see page 10). These are important in selecting activities for your plan – although for information on doing a more detailed risk assessment, see the upcoming section 'Risk identification and analysis' (page 70). As a reminder, these were:

1. *Reputational risk*: the risk that your project/policy will backfire due to inadequate engagement
2. *Confrontational risk*: the risk that your engagement will turn sour due to inadequate planning or facilitation.

When faced with a situation of high reputational risk – particularly if a policy or service will have a significant economic or social impact – you will likely benefit from, and/or be mandated to do, a lot of engagement. And you are likely to be encouraged to pursue engagement techniques that allow participants to have more involvement in, and impact on, outcomes.

If a policy or program does have a significant economic or social impact, that often goes hand-in-hand with an increased likelihood that there will be opposing views on what the outcome should be, or how it is to be arrived at, and the people involved will be heavily invested in their views. When this is the case, you have a high confrontational risk.

Both types of risk influence the types of techniques that it will be most helpful to select for your project. We have mapped our techniques against both types of risk in Figure 14 (see overleaf).

Figure 14: Engagement activities sorted by relationship to risk

Risk of conflict	Need to reduce reputational risk		
	Low	**Medium**	**High**
High	» Consultative interview » Factsheet » Polling » Information kit » Televoting	» Factsheet » Advertising » 1800 numbers » Information kit » Media event » Trade show or exhibition	» Citizens' panel » Deliberative polling » Focus group » Collaborative problem definition » Community mapping » Unconference » Polling » Survey » Bilateral meeting » Community or public meeting » Computer–assisted participation » Consensus conference » Consensus forum » Issues conference » Search conference » Televoting
Medium	» Online discussion group » Interactive e-conferencing » Issues conference	» Deliberative polling » Roundtable » Collaborative problem definition » Community mapping » Unconference » Advertising » Community or public meeting » Computer–assisted participation » Consensus conference	» Charrette » Policy wiki » Citizens' jury
Low	» Nominal group process » Media event » Trade show or exhibition	» Ideas challenge	» Search conference

Note that the table in Figure 14 uses reputational risk from the perspective of how important it is for you to lower the risk, rather than a simple measure of the risk level itself. This is because a high reputational risk doesn't in itself reduce the applicability of certain techniques. A factsheet, for example, can be useful in high and low reputational risk scenarios. However, it may do little to reduce the likelihood of a negative outcome in a high reputational risk scenario. On the other hand, a collaborative or deliberate process (if well executed) may be very useful in reducing your reputational risk by improving your stakeholder reach or the quality of your recommendations.

Doing it yourself

Often, you won't have much of a budget to throw around for hiring facilitators and the like. If you're in this situation, it's helpful to know which activities you can realistically deliver yourself. In order to assist with this, we've marked each technique with the key skill required to deliver it. If this says 'Expert', it's best to avoid trying to run the activity yourself unless you have prior experience doing so. Otherwise, these skills tend to fall into two categories: 'Facilitator' and 'Communicator':

» *Facilitator*: Do you feel comfortable leading a group? Have you worked with groups before and know how to spot people who haven't contributed and encourage them to talk? Do you feel confident negotiating minor conflicts and making sure everyone feels heard so they can move past or resolve issues? If you can answer 'yes' to all these questions, you're in a good position to handle these techniques with a bit of reading and planning.

» *Communicator*: Are you an excellent writer or speaker? Do people understand you easily, even if they have differing levels of education or knowledge? If so, you shouldn't have any trouble delivering the techniques for which this skill is required.

Planning for reporting

Engagement reports are seldom completed at the end of a policy or service project. This means, of course, that the public and other stakeholders are unable to determine or understand to what degree their interests have been taken into consideration. By planning to report, and having a frame for this from the outset, your overheads can be lowered and the transparency of the engagements significantly improved.

Since we now have a strong frame for our plan, we also have the frame for our report. This means that if you keep a copy of your engagement plan, and you frequently return to it to update each round with the outcomes as you have them, then by the time your project has been completed it should only take a matter of hours to finish the engagement report. How does this compare with how you do things today? The Scaffle online application makes this even easier by keeping your engagement plan online in an easy-to-update-and-export format.

Completing our example

We now have a complete design for our engagement project, and a clear understanding of how each step will build on and support our policy design.

3. Define and prioritise solutions:

    a. Engagement: 6 weeks, 1 July – 12 Aug (50%)

    b. Outcome 1: Exploring – develop a range of feasible solutions; get insight into stakeholder perceptions of options

        i. Engagement activity 1: Search conference (for broad range of ideas)

        ii. Engagement activity 2: Charrette (for targetting development of ideas)

    d. Outcome 2: Prioritising – comparative analysis of solutions; surface any known tensions about the proposed options

        i. Engagement activity 3: Deliberative polling (gauge citizen sentiment)

        ii. Engagement activity 4: Bipartisan mettings (check in with key stakeholders)

    c. Output: Draft and get approval for options paper

4. Draft recommendations report:

    a. Engagement: 3 weeks, 27 Aug – 16 Sept (30%)

    b. Outcome 3: Communicating – ensure all stakeholders know we have a draft recommendation

        i. Engagement activity 5: Press release

    c. Outcome 4: Confirming – surface and resolve tensions; clarify details of the recommendation

        ii. Engagement activity 6: Community meeting

> d. Draft and get approval for recommendations paper
>
>> iii. Engagement activity 7: Delphi process (for co-drafting)

5. Confirm final recommendations:

   a. Engagement: 2 weeks, 1–14 Oct (20%)

   b. Outcome 5: Communicating – ensure all stakeholders know we have a final recommendation; let stakeholders know what will happen next

      i. Engagement activity: Advertising

   c. Outcome 6: Confirming – finalise any last details

      i. Engagement activity: Call for submissions

   d. Outcome 7: Scanning – gauge likely reactions

      ii. Engagement activity: Focus group

   c. Draft and get approval for final recommendations paper

6. Implement solution (proposed to commence 1 Jan)

7. Measure and review (schedule 12 months from 1 Jan)

What might've taken days to design has been mapped out in a number of hours. While there are probably still some parts that will need refinement, we have quickly established a design that, with a little formatting, can be taken into a meeting to discuss.

Because of the planning process we've gone through, we will also automatically avoid many of the common mistakes made in engagement, which we discussed in Part One of this book. We will also be able to report confidently and efficiently on what engagements we have done, and why.

Planning and running an engagement activity

In this section, we provide an overview of the basic steps you can expect to undertake as you plan and run each of your engagement activities. This is a starting point, to be used in combination with more-detailed information specific to the techniques themselves. There is a wealth of such information available on the internet – it would not be practical to replicate it here. Ideally, try to learn about each technique from people who have experience with it, as this will give you the best results and help you to avoid 'beginner' mistakes. In Part Four, we have included links to resources we found useful in compiling this text, to point you in the right direction.

In general, the process of designing, running and integrating the results of an engagement can be summarised as shown in Figure 15.

Figure 15: Engagement process

1. Frame → **2. Design** → **3. Run** → **4. Understand** → **5. Report**

EVENT PLAN   DATA FOR ANALYSIS   SYNTHESISED INFO REPORT

Source: Adapted from Office of Citizens and Civics (2006)

1. Frame

To start planning your engagement activity, clearly state its objective and how it will contribute to the broader process (Sheedy, 2008). It may be helpful to articulate specific goals, and any contextual information that is relevant to this activity or its objective. You should also be as specific as possible about who you will engage and why they are the right group/s. This is valuable information to capture directly in your main report, as it will be good to have easy access to it once all your engagement activities are complete – it can easily be forgotten. Start a planning document for each activity so that you can keep track of the specifics and capture all of your to-dos and logistics.

2. Design

Design is the nitty-gritty of how an activity will be delivered. You should complete this stage with a level of detail that will fully prepare you for running the activity – this may be as granular as a minuted runsheet if you are taking on the facilitation yourself. In doing so, be sure to consider the following points.

Who will run the activity?

Running a good event typically requires that a few roles are filled. In some cases, you may be able to assign each of these to a separate person. In others, you may take on multiple roles yourself, which might include the following:

» *A stager*: someone who takes care of setting up and getting the room ready. They will need to consider how the space will impact the event. They'll be looking for anything that might make participants feel less comfortable and address this. For example, if the room is messy, they'll tidy it. If it has no windows, they might try to find a plant for a table. Or they'll make sure there's water or other refreshments at hand. These seemingly small details can have a big impact on how willing people are to engage with you and open up.

» *A host*: someone who makes sure that everyone feels comfortable, like they belong when they arrive. This could involve anything from confirming participants are in the right space and letting them know when you'll start, through to thoughtfully introducing them to others so that they begin to engage in conversation. A host can help everyone to begin your engagement in an open and comfortable frame of mind.

» *A facilitator*: the person who will lead the group through the engagement process. This person obviously needs to be able to lead, but they must also fade into the background as participants start talking. They should maintain an even and appreciative demeanour, even when under attack. To defuse a situation, they will naturally redirect participant frustrations into answering related questions. They will also make sure everyone has an equal opportunity to contribute and to feel heard (these are not always the same thing). They listen for when participants show expertise and call on those people at the right time if the group doesn't naturally notice that expertise. They'll keep the group on track and ensure that the conversation contributes to the desired objectives.

» *A time cop*: someone who makes sure that the facilitator knows when the time allocated to a task is nearly up, so that they can prepare to switch to the next task and keep the day on track.

» *A point of contact*: the person whom participants should contact if they have any questions before or after the event.

Whether you have to do it all yourself or bring in expert help, think through the aforementioned roles as you plan the event. This might just mean you remember to arrive early enough to set up the room, or that you're ready by the door to greet everyone as they arrive rather than hiding behind a computer at the front of the room. Give thought to how you'll make sure all these tasks are managed, and if you're working with a team, be explicit about who will do what. This stands even if your engagement isn't an in-person one. How do visitors know what to do when they arrive at a webinar or at your website? Are they overloaded with information or is it an easy experience? How are they led through the process? Do they know how to ask for help? How long will it all take? The same principles apply because all participants have the same needs: to feel comfortable; to trust you; to understand your expectations; and to feel heard, whether they are on the other side of a monitor, the other end of a phone line, or in the room.

Speaking their language

Research your stakeholders ahead of time. Learn how they talk about the issue at hand. Is there specific jargon they use or seem to avoid? Do they use the same phrasing you do, or do they frame things differently? You want to be relatable, so you should understand how they talk about things, even if you choose not to use their words yourself – these could be either inappropriate or undesirable in certain situations, such as when working with young people or in culturally sensitive environments. It's okay to use your language, but it can help to soften it for your audience, particularly if you tend to be overly formal. It can also be a way to open up and be transparent about wanting to better understand the stakeholders. For example, you may have the opportunity to ask what a word or phrase means to them, in their context: 'I'd really like to understand what you mean when you say that the event was "cool". Do you mean that it was a fun place to be or that there were people there who you looked up to?'

Likewise, knowing what not to say is very important. For example, find out how your stakeholders like to be addressed. Some women don't take issue with being part of a group who are addressed collectively as 'guys'. Other women, however, take particular offence at this colloquialism. By chatting with your stakeholders in advance about anything that you should specifically avoid saying or need to phrase carefully, you will avoid having an innocent mistake ruin your engagement.

Selecting your participants

Ideally, you will know who your broad stakeholder group is before you select your activity. But now you need to get specific to determine whom you'll invite and how you'll invite them. Three methods are typical for selecting or recruiting stakeholders for an engagement activity:

» *purposive* – hand-select representatives who you already know, or who you find through research, such as across social media or special-interest forums

» *random* – use census/postal/other data to randomly invite a specific number of participants (remember that many will cancel/decline, so invite more than you need)

» *self-elective* – advertise your engagement and allow anyone with an interest to opt in.

Each option will achieve a different result for your engagement.

Purposive selection may enable deeper conversations due to the higher degree of trust between you and the participants, which means it's best for when you need to dive deep into an issue or design something collaboratively. Usually, this is the fastest and cheapest way to get stakeholders together. However, it's unlikely to be representative and may invite inherent biases that are similar to your own.

Random selection is best for providing information that can be extrapolated out to a broader group – useful if you need to make a case for a course of action with evidence that is more representative. This can be the most costly approach, depending on your access to stakeholder information, such as addresses. You may need to contract an external group to source participants on your behalf, which can cost anywhere between $10 and $250 (or even more) per person.

Self-elective selection ensures that the most passionate people are in the room, which is helpful if you need to understand the strongest proponents/opponents and their views and interactions. This can be cheaper than random selection, as your costs will be limited to where and how you advertise. However, you are unlikely to get participants who are representative. They are more likely to be strongly aligned with one side of the issue or the other.

Take a look at your objectives when weighing up these benefits to determine what will work best for you. See the section 'Stakeholder identification and capability assessment' (page 71) for more techniques and tips on finding and understanding stakeholders.

Logistics

Ideally, note down what requirements your stakeholders are likely to have before you start determining your specific where-and-when-type considerations. For example, will you need to work around school hours? Do the participants need access to public transport? Do they need to be reimbursed for their time? Will they trust you, or would a mediator be more appropriate? If you can't answer these questions yourself, talk to someone among your stakeholders, or who knows them very well: anyone who can fill you in on these details. Use this to help you find the right location, rather than finding a location first and expecting the participants to come to you. The stakeholders themselves might be able to make some good recommendations here, so don't let a lack of budget block your creativity. Often, passionate stakeholders can help you find a location within their networks that is free or cheap. Be cautious, however, if your issue is highly polarised -- your choice of location or timing may be perceived as enabling or preferencing one side or another.

Communications

Plan your communications ahead of time for before and after your engagement. This could be a lot of work, requiring the involvement of your communications team, or you might need to do just enough to source and inform your participants. It really depends on your project. The higher its profile, the more lead time you'll need to allow for crafting communications and all the appropriate sign-offs. If you're managing a large project, you'll need to prepare variations of your communications for different audiences, possibly in multiple languages – this can be very time-consuming. Also, as the public face of your engagement, you're likely to have your comms team asking for changes that conflict with those that other influential people are suggesting. It'll be a bit of a balancing act, requiring plenty of creativity and tenacity. Be prepared to pick your battles, and keep the aim of your communications in mind.

If you're recruiting participants using the self-elective method, make sure your call to action doesn't become so diluted with government jargon that your stakeholders won't understand it. Testing variants of a communication with your stakeholders can provide evidence for why you should or shouldn't use particular language or content.

Creating timelines and runsheets

You'll need a timeline for your event as well as a runsheet, to make sure that everything goes according to plan. These two documents serve different purposes.

A *timeline* provides a detailed view of all the activities required in the lead-up to, and in the wake of, an engagement. Usually, this is broken down at a daily level.

A *runsheet* documents everything that will happen during your engagement, potentially to the minute. Make sure you include time for introductions, ice-breakers, and appropriate breaks for food or comfort. Runsheets may not be as important for online, self-driven engagements such as surveys. But in these cases, you should still review the experience from the perspective of a user and run through it a few times yourself, to catch anything that might cause a participant to stumble.

Preparing your materials

Engagements can require all sorts of material, such as presentations, speeches, Post-it Notes, pens, printouts and so on. Sometimes, the time needed to get everything together can catch you off guard at the last minute. For example, if you need any specialist printing done externally, allow at least a week's lead time. Make sure that you allow for enough time to get everything together.

Planning for using the outputs

Make sure you take time during your design stage to figure out how to take the information/output from your engagement and use it to contribute meaningfully to your project. Having a great, generative day of conversations might be lovely, but if you're left with 3000 sticky notes that don't make any sense removed from the context of the day, you'll be relying on your memory to write up the outputs. And if the outputs don't match what the participants themselves took away from the day, those people may be frustrated or disappointed.

Many good engagements follow a format of opening up to all the possibilities and then progressively narrowing in on a point. This might be achieved through the ordering of questions, or helping participants find and name themes. However, some formats do not allow you to create a logical and progressive order, such as when participants are responding in isolation. In these instances, look for ways in which you can plan ahead of time to make the grouping and ordering easier yourself. For example, if you're seeking ideas, you might let participants nominate a category their idea fits into, such as 'infrastructural' or 'social'.

In general, be realistic in your planning, and allow enough time for this step to do it properly both before and after your activity. Drawing out the representative insights and applying them appropriately requires time and focus.

Evaluation and learning

How will you know if your activity is a success? What metrics are appropriate for helping you to learn and be better next time? At a minimum, plan some time for yourself and/or your team to get together after the engagement to discuss how it went. Did you get the outputs you were expecting? If you used an external facilitator, did they perform as expected? How did the stakeholders perceive the engagement? Did you even ask them? How easy was it to make the outputs useful to the project? How could this all be better next time?

If you can, capture what you learn somewhere that other teams might be able to make use of it. Consider writing an internal blog or using some other media to share your experience.

3. Run

This is the delivery of your engagement activity. For any technique, there are core aspects of the facilitation of the activity that should be addressed.

Setting ground rules

Let participants know what you're asking of them and what they are not allowed to do. This is part of being transparent and making people feel safe in contributing. Boundaries are important in the sense of providing permission for people to act, as much as restricting their behaviour.

Hosting and facilitating

Decide ahead of time how you will greet participants and welcome them to your process. This might be done through the language of a landing page if your engagement is delivered online, or a dedicated greeter for an in-person event. This approach extends to the facilitation style. Will you make sure everyone gets a fair turn, or will you allow the participants to self-organise? Let participants know what your style is going to be, so that they don't make assumptions about why you are more or less heavy-handed.

Support throughout the process

Ensure you get the best out of the participants by assisting them in building their knowledge, capability and/or efficacy as appropriate to your process. Consider if resources such as subject-matter experts are useful in helping participants to explore an idea. Also, be conscious of the fact that participants are likely to bring their own baggage to your engagement. If you are aware of any tensions that are directly or indirectly related to your process, make sure to allow time for 'venting' so that this tension can be released and participants can focus on the task at hand.

Communicating the impact

Let participants know which part of your broader project they are impacting and how you plan to make use of their input. This can influence the type of feedback they give you, as they will be less likely to make assumptions about what you are asking of them. It also gives them confidence that what you are asking will meaningfully contribute to the outcomes.

Further contributions and communication

Ensure the participants know how to get updates on your project, and whether there will be an opportunity for them to be involved again in the future.

4. Understand

Before you can integrate all of the great information you got from your engagement, you need to make sense of it. Even if people were directly collaborating on a policy during your activity, there will be a point of review when you'll need to stop and ask yourself, 'What are people saying? What does it mean? Does this help answer our questions?'. Sometimes, the engagement may produce more issues that need to be explored. You may want to plan a new engagement to help resolve these if you were expecting that you'd get more conclusions than questions.

You might find yourself with a large amount of qualitative data and a great sense of community after an event, but have no idea about how to make sure it all feeds back into the policy or service design project. Start by looking for patterns. Can you highlight sentences in different transcripts or group sticky notes that seem to be on the same theme? It can be helpful to physically cut out the sentences, or copy them into a new document where you can group them. If feasible, keep track of who said what, in case you want to use any of the quotes later on. Once you've created as many themes as is reasonable, you can start your analysis. Look for connections between the themes. Which have the most support? What does this tell you about your project? How can you use the themes and the support for them to synthesise recommendations for your project? This process can be time-consuming but it is extremely worthwhile. Often, the results won't be quite what you expected!

5. Report

Once you've got your outcomes and you've integrated the feedback into your project, you'll need to report on the outcomes. You might do this for each activity or after a set of related activities. You'll need to report what you recommended, how this decision was made, and who influenced the final decision. Ideally, you'll report at two levels – to decision-makers and to participants – before more generally reflecting on your process.

Reporting to decision-makers

Decision-makers are most interested in what your recommendations are and how your process provides evidence for the validity of those recommendations. This evidence includes:

» who you engaged, who was left out, and why

» how this selection represents the relevant constituency

» the result – recommendations for the project/policy, learnings about stakeholder sentiment and risks, and so on.

Reporting to stakeholders

Stakeholders are interested in similar things to decision-makers. However, they typically have a greater focus on self, including how they had an impact on the outcomes. They might want to know:

» who else you engaged (if not just them)

» how the information or evidence led to the recommendations

» whether any themes or outcomes were more influential than others

» what didn't make it into the recommendations, even though it was supported, and why/why not.

Evaluating your process

You should also regularly assess the quality of your process. This can help you to improve it next time, particularly if you're managing the facilitation yourself. You can do this with participants either at the end of the engagement activity or at the end of the project. Ask direct questions regarding:

» the quality of the facilitation

» whether the information provided was helpful to the process

» whether a variety of perspectives was heard and discussed in a respectful and equitable way

» whether prior expectations of the potential for impact were met

» whether participants' trust in the process was increased.

This information could be included in a final report for the engagement project, to demonstrate the care with which you conducted your process from beginning to end.

Why it's best to engage from the outset

While you can't always plan engagement from the very start of a policy or service design project, there are some big advantages to be had when you can. The earliest points of planning and research have a significant effect on how a problem is framed and therefore how it will be resolved. While it may be slightly different for service design projects, it still holds that the more engagement that occurs in planning and research, the better the outcome.

This may seem counterintuitive to those public servants who are used to rushing through the early stages of a project in order to get it moving and signed off. While there is a first level of design and planning that is naturally needed in order to start the ball rolling, it is worth revisiting this in the first round of the engagement to check any assumptions that were made and deepen the understanding of the problem space. At Collabforge, we think of this as 'slowing down to speed up'. This means that, while it can feel a little painful to invite others to question your design decisions, taking the time to do this up-front means that later on you can pick up pace with confidence, knowing that it's far less likely that a critical aspect has been missed.

There's no such thing as engaging too early – it's just that who you speak to might be different. As soon as the need for an intervention has been triggered, whether through policy or some other means, you'll be talking to people to gain information about the problem and the means of solving it; that is, whether a policy is required, or a review of a policy or service/program, or some other intervention. Keeping a record – and being mindful – of these conversations later allows you to provide the reasoning or evidence for why a particular course of action was taken. Customer–client relationship management (CRM) tools or planning apps like Scaffle can be helpful in tracking these interactions – relating to the particular individuals in the case of CRMs, or to your engagement process in the Scaffle app.

If your project has a clear starting point and you have followed the steps in the Scaffle method to arrive at your engagement plan, you are in a perfect position to start getting others involved. Getting stakeholders (internal or external) to review or provide details for your plan will assist you in spotting gaps and getting a better outcome for your project. This is a perfect time for collaboration as well. You're not claiming to have all the answers at this point, and you're not trying to solve the problem yet either. The rules of the game and the players can still be changed at this stage.

Important areas that others can help you with, to make sure you start strong, are:

» contextual analysis

» risk identification

» stakeholder identification.

Contextual analysis

You're probably pretty familiar with the notion of doing some research when you commence a new policy or service project. This might include looking at local statistics, or even commissioning surveys or focus groups. What you might be less familiar with is treating this step as an opportunity for engagement.

When you're undertaking a contextual analysis for a project, who better to help you get a clear picture than your stakeholders? Without the experience of those on the ground, it may be hard for you to discover:

» what has been done in this space before, especially by groups outside your organisation

» if there are any conflicts between stakeholders

» how your organisation is perceived by stakeholders.

This information can be important for confirming your engagement plan. If your organisation is perceived very poorly, you may need to consider outside help to ensure your engagement appears impartial.

Engaging with stakeholders to map and explore economic, social, environmental, technological and political influence factors (State of Victoria, 2005) can be a particularly worthwhile exercise. You can establish facts that will be critical in determining your policy or service project outcomes, as well as improving and customising your engagement plan for your unique audiences.

Engagement techniques particularly suited to this purpose include:

» collaborative problem definition

» community mapping

» unconference

» bilateral meetings

» community or public meeting

» consensus forum

» issues conference

» search conference.

Risk identification and analysis

You might not need to create a risk assessment for your project, but your project will benefit if you do. This is a great activity in which to involve stakeholders. Experts and other stakeholders will be able to see your project from different angles than you can. You could just focus on engagement risks, or on risks relating to your broader project. If your project is small, you might just create a combined list of risks. If it's large, it may be best to separate out the risks regarding your engagement performing as planned, from your policy or service delivery and implementation risks.

Here are some examples of potential risks relating to your stakeholders that you could mitigate through your engagement planning:

» stakeholders delay project due to unmet concerns

» stakeholders introduce additional cost or scope that was unknown at project planning stage

» stakeholders fight with each other

» regulatory authority stakeholders are slow to grant approval

» regulatory authority stakeholders add cost – require additional studies etc

» regulatory authority stakeholders do not approve the project

» stakeholders ignore project communications

» stakeholders you need to re-engage stop responding to you

» project sponsor/organisation doesn't approve of design/plan

» stakeholders do not receive sufficient communication to understand your expectations or contribute in a meaningful way

» project sponsor/executives are not aware of project progress

» regulatory authority stakeholders are not contacted early enough and cause problems as a result (Roseke, 2015).

Other risk areas to consider getting engagement on include:

» occupational health and safety risks – Are participants/staff exposed to any danger at the engagement events?

» ethical risks – Is the engagement inclusive, honest, respectful, equitable and justified?

» legal risks – Is anything being promised that cannot be delivered?

» reputational risks – How might the engagement do more damage than good?

» environmental risks – Could the engagement activities cause any physical damage?

Techniques that can be useful in uncovering and analysing your risks include:

» roundtable

» advisory committee, board or council

» codesign process

» charrette

» bilateral meetings

» community or public meeting

» survey

» focus group.

Stakeholder identification and capability assessment

Some of your stakeholders will be apparent and easy to reach. Others will require more work to identify and connect with. It is easy to fail to identify stakeholders due to your own biases or blind spots. You can overcome these by working early on with your easy-to-reach stakeholders, to get help in identifying the harder-to-reach or harder-to-know audiences. An additional bonus of asking for this help is that the stakeholders you work with will often be more willing than they might otherwise be to open up their personal networks as a source of further stakeholder contacts – particularly if your efforts to involve others are motivated by a genuine interest in finding the best possible outcome.

Having a framework with which to map and analyse stakeholders helps you identify where you have gaps, such as who may have been forgotten by your project. It is best to look at this problem from a number of angles, to reduce the risk that you miss a key group. Mayers (2005, p. 6) suggests taking several approaches, including:

» identification by knowledgeable individuals

» identification through issue-relevant records, either in the public record or sourced through related agencies or knowledgeable individuals

» self-selection – directly advertising to attract interested stakeholders

» identification and verification by other stakeholders.

Mayers further suggests (p. 6) that the key questions to be asked in relation to the above approaches are as follows:

» Who are the potential beneficiaries?

» Who might be adversely affected?

» Who has existing rights?

» Who is likely to be voiceless?

» Who is likely to resent change and mobilise resistance against it?

» Who is responsible for the intended plans?

» Who has money, skills or key information?

» Whose behaviour has to change for success?

Figure 16: Rainbow diagram for stakeholder identification

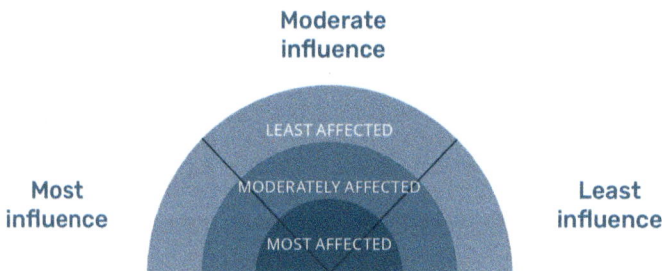

Source: Chevalier & Buckles (2008), p. 171

Any number of tools are available for mapping and analysing stakeholders. Figure 16 comprises a simple framework by Chevalier and Buckles (2008) – adapted from Mayers' work – that you could use when working with others to map and understand your stakeholders. It explores issues of power and affectedness but is designed to be easily adapted according to the criteria of interest to your project – you can add or reduce the segments or rings as appropriate. The key thing is that, by starting to build a picture of where your known stakeholders sit in relation to each other, you'll naturally create gaps. Asking if anyone fills these gaps is a simple way of ensuring you don't miss stakeholders.

Your role in addressing power dynamics

Stakeholders may contribute unevenly to a project for reasons beyond simply their political power or influence. They may be critical to your decision-making process but need assistance to better understand the issue, frame their response, or address some other gap in capability or efficacy. Consider what your role should be in enabling stakeholders, and how able they are to begin with. You may need to devote some time to helping them get a clearer perspective or understand the issues in play, in order to provide you with useable information. Working with stakeholders in an educative fashion can also help you discover what types of messaging and which messages are most appropriate when you're communicating with a broader group later on. For example, by helping a representative group come to a different perspective on an issue through providing information and resources they wouldn't otherwise have been able to access, you might discover which of those resources are the most effective in making the case for them, and tailor public communications to reinforce or educate on those specific points (rather than all of them).

Techniques that can help with stakeholder identification or analysis-focused engagement include:

- » process codesign
- » advisory committee, board or council
- » community mapping
- » bilateral meetings
- » community or public meeting
- » collaborative problem definition.

Testing/checking your plan

You've already mapped out your engagement plan, and, with the help of your stakeholders, you're ahead of the game in establishing your project context, risks and key stakeholders. This is the perfect time to engage the stakeholders to review your plan as a whole. They can help ensure your plan is reflective of the information that they have provided to date. They can also help you spot any areas where you might be missing particular stakeholders or have overlooked a potential risk.

It can feel uncomfortable to open up your planning to stakeholders. This is best handled by cautiously selecting stakeholders from whom to seek advice. Look for those with whom you have good relationships and who represent the interests of key stakeholder groups. If you have identified any stakeholders who pose risks if not given adequate opportunities for engagement, those are usually important ones to seek feedback from. For example, if you have representatives of marginalised stakeholders in the mix, try to get their feedback on your plan. They can give you good advice on whether your plan will give stakeholders who are similar to themselves an adequate opportunity to provide input. They can also give you pointers on running your activities, to make sure vulnerable groups are engaged in a way that is respectful, authentic, and makes them feel safe enough to contribute.

Bringing it all together

By this point, you will have realised that there is a lot of information to keep track of in planning, recording and reporting on your engagement project. It definitely helps if you set up a system involving documents and a simple file structure on your computer that matches your plan, so you can quickly locate key information. For example, you might keep your master engagement plan document in a project folder, then create a sub-folder for each round of engagement, and another folder within those for each engagement activity. The Scaffle app enables you to store documents or files within the main master plan for easy reference. This can be especially helpful if you need to keep track of the latest version of a document or collaborate within a team.

This section has walked you through how to outline your entire engagement project, then start filling in the gaps. However, as you get into the details, you will likely find that you need more help, such as someone who can assist you in tackling a very specific scenario, or someone who can provide information based on first-hand experience that you're lacking. Collaboration, particularly with your colleagues, is usually critical in addressing these types of challenges, and delivering an effective project in general. Part Three of this book gives you specific advice on planning for and delivering collaboration, whether as part of your engagement activities or to get the most out of your teamwork.

3 Delivering great collaboration

Collaboration, done well and at the right time, can improve the definition of policy problems and the development of solutions. It can also reduce risk and deliver stronger levels of shared understanding, buy-in and even voluntary compliance. As the expression goes, 'Those who write the plan don't fight the plan'. However, there is often a lack of clarity surrounding what collaboration is, when to use it and how to best do it. This confusion can increase when considering how newer terminology fits into the mix, such as codesign, design thinking, and cocreation.

Collabforge founder Dr Mark Elliott developed the 3Cs framework for collaboration 15 years ago, as part of his PhD, to help bring clarity to this issue. Collabforge has since developed this framework through hundreds of projects with governments and public sector organisations. It provides specific ways of understanding and doing collaboration that are easy to grasp and apply – and, when done well, deliver consistently positive results.

This part of the book provides a summary of this framework and methodology.

What is collaboration?

At the heart of Dr Elliott's 3Cs framework is the recognition that collaboration comprises three interrelated social processes (see Figure 17 overleaf):

1. cocreation – a number of people together creating new ideas, things, decisions and so on

2. cooperation – groups or individuals contributing to a process that aggregates value

3. coordination – bringing people or things together in a way that identifies patterns.

Figure 17: The 3Cs framework

Cocreation
Add / edit / delete rights to a
shared pool of content

⬆

Cooperation
Individual contributions to a
process that aggregates for gain

⬆

Coordination
Individual elements brought into a
space that foregrounds patterns

The three processes illustrated in Figure 17 are interdependent, each providing the enabling conditions for the others. Coordination provides the foundation that enables cooperation, with cooperation then making cocreation possible. So while these three processes do take place individually, they are always happening together. For example, several people may sit together in a meeting and cocreate the goals and approach for an engagement project. But as they do so, they will be using cooperative, turn-taking approaches to build on their ideas through conversation, while also relying on the coordination of a shared language.

Understanding the distinctions between these interrelated processes allows you to more clearly determine which social process is occurring or should be planned for, with which stakeholders, and what you need to support them.

Coordination

Coordination happens when potentially unrelated things or people are drawn together into a space that foregrounds patterns or relationships. These patterns and relationships allow the participants, or the group as a whole, to act with new-found intelligence. Coordination doesn't rely on explicit interactions between people to be effective.

A classic example of coordination is how a great conference gathers diverse people in a structured environment to bring about 'designed serendipity'. The coordination aspect of bringing people together for a conference evidences a relationship between you and the people around you. You share a common interest you might not otherwise have been aware of – if you were just passing in the street, for example. As a result of this coordination, you might find yourself randomly chatting with someone you're seated next to and marvelling at the great connection you've just made.

Cooperation

Like coordination, cooperation does not rely on participants explicitly interacting with one another. Instead, they can interact via a process that links their contributions to form a larger, aggregate outcome. Unlike coordination, however, cooperation has an active level of participation and requires compliance with a shared process.

As a simple example, consider an electronic survey of 1000 people on a particular topic. Participants contribute their responses to the survey without interacting with one another, and the process of aggregating those responses and compiling a result links the contributions into a greater whole. In this example, compliance with the process is in the form of the channel of submission. If a participant wants to submit their response by writing it on the sidewalk, odds are it won't make it into the aggregated result.

Cocreation – the heart of collaboration

Cocreation, on the other hand, requires direct engagement with content (as opposed to a process). It also requires direct engagement with other people. This is because to create something new, multiple inputs have to be made to a common 'pool of content'. Individual contributions almost always influence the contributions of others. As a result, social interaction is needed to negotiate these contributions and the resulting changes to the final outcome.

Examples of cocreation range from large, complex tasks such as policy development and the co-authoring of a document, to day-to-day activities such as developing ideas with co-workers on a whiteboard or even through conversation. In all of these cases, the central point is that something new is created by merging inputs from multiple participants. This does not happen with cooperation, where the inputs aren't merged but remain independent (even in aggregation).

For most people, the coming together of these three processes – cocreation, cooperation and coordination – is what they associate with collaboration. And the more cocreation that is involved, the more it feels like 'genuine collaboration'. Because of the depth of interaction required for effective cocreation, at Collabforge, *we see cocreation as the heart of collaboration.*

What does this mean for collaborative engagement?

Typically, all engagements have aspects of coordination, cooperation and cocreation, whether you explicitly plan them or not.

There will be some level of coordination between stakeholders and the beneficiary of the engagement, for example. This may take the form of communication to the community about policy changes, or reporting the outcomes of engagement up the chain. Cooperation, meanwhile, will be evident in most forms of engagement, such as when community members are asked to respond to a survey, or to provide feedback on a policy position paper.

Because cocreation opens up access to a shared pool of content for direct influence, it is most prominent within the engagement delivery team itself. As a result, for almost all significant or complex engagements, cocreation takes place during the planning stages – with or without external stakeholders.

By learning to think in this way about the work you are doing, you'll be able to quickly identify engagement that, while claiming to be collaborative, is not really collaborative. Inviting participants to create sticky notes about their ideas, for example, isn't really collaborative unless their work is integrated into a new and better outcome. If this negotiation and merging is happening elsewhere, without ongoing dialogue with those who contributed, while you might have achieved excellent coordination and cooperation, you will fall short of cocreation. This might be okay in most situations, but it will ring false to those who feel they were promised a greater level of influence, and create a negative response to whatever is ultimately delivered.

Designing and delivering great collaboration – the Collabforge method

The Collabforge method described here is a summarised version of the larger, more detailed methodology that will be presented in Dr Mark Elliott's forthcoming book on collaboration. This methodology was developed through more than a decade of work and some 500 projects with the public sector.

While the following steps are sequential from a planning perspective, once you are into the actual process of delivering a collaborative project, you will need to revisit past steps as you prepare for or take new ones. For example, after Cocreate (step 3: working with a group to create your first shared outcomes), you may need to revisit Convene (step 2: bringing people together for the first time) if you discover there are other people you should involve. Because of the interplay between the steps, it can be useful to also consider them general principles for collaboration.

Step 1: Decide

Make the decision: Should you collaborate?

Collaboration can deliver difference-making buy-in and support, as well as breakthrough capability and solutions. However, it requires time and commitment, and it can introduce the risk of conflict if it's not resourced appropriately. This applies equally to collaboration during the planning and delivery phases, as well as to your team and stakeholders. So making the conscious decision to collaborate is the most important first step in great collaboration design. When you do this, you exert significantly more influence on the outcome, as it forces you to weigh up the expected costs and benefits.

Going through this process will enable you to form a hypothesis about the potential for collaboration in your context – what the opportunity might be, who should be involved, under what premise, and so on. Collaborative processes can be hard and require a lot of energy, especially at the beginning. Knowing exactly what you want to get out of the collaboration is important, both for your own and your team's motivation, and in justifying the time and resources needed to make it succeed.

How to make your decision

Whatever criteria you use, the key point with this step is to make a conscious decision that is informed by some amount of deliberation – and ideally, you will not be the only person involved in this deliberation. Carefully consider the pros and cons of collaboration.

If you need a quick indication of whether or not collaboration is right for your situation, just answer these three questions:

1. Is the problem you're trying to solve one that benefits from collaboration?
2. Do you have the authority and capability to convene your collaboration?
3. Is there goodwill on all sides to forge a shared resolution to the problem?

The next few sections offer more information about each of these questions and how to answer them.

Problems that benefit from collaboration

It's reasonable to assume that, since you are engaging with stakeholders, you alone cannot deliver the impact required or answer the questions that need to be addressed. However, in many situations, you might be able to get the input you need through non-collaborative processes. Collaboration is best suited to solving problems that are complex, have resisted being solved in the past, have many interdependent elements, or require especially creative or out-of-the-box thinking. If your project involves any or all of these factors, it will probably need more than just consultation to get a great outcome. Projects with these criteria are good candidates for collaborative engagement, as their hard-to-solve features justify the resources and energy needed to form and run a collaboration.

Having the means, authority and capability to collaborate

To deliver a collaborative process, you must have the means, authority and capability to bring together the necessary participants. You also need to be able to keep any promises you make to participants – such as that you will implement their designs, if that is the purpose of the collaboration. The closer you are to those who will 'own' the decision on, and implementation of, a policy or service, the more authority and capability you have. Without this, it will fall to the perception of the value and urgency of the solution within your authorising environment to determine what you can do and promise. Conversations about your ability to get the right people in the room, and to convert their work into actions, are best had up-front so that you can be transparent and not overcommit. If you don't have the required means or authority, a deliberative level of involvement may be more appropriate, one that provides a good level of interaction while allowing you to retain a greater degree of control over outcomes.

What goodwill means for a collaboration

Goodwill is important because it drives trust; it's the grease that keeps collaboration from grinding to a halt when tensions arise. Before convening a collaboration, have direct conversations with some of the people you would like to involve. This will give you a sense of their willingness to collaborate and/or compromise on a solution. They don't need to necessarily be on the same side of an issue, or agree beforehand, but an interest in sharing in the process is important. Conversely, you should also take note of individuals or organisations who have, or who might spark, ill will due to their personalities, biases, or general external perceptions. The level of goodwill or ill will present at the outset isn't in itself a reason to decide to collaborate or not, but it will be a key factor in how hard or easy the job will be and therefore should be considered in your decision. The higher the degree of ill will, the more resource-intensive and time-consuming the process will be. It may also ultimately fail despite all your best efforts. If your reputational risk is extremely high, you may want to proceed anyway, but do so cautiously, seeking collaborative techniques that focus on facts or shared points of agreement, such as consensus forums or collaborative problem definition. Otherwise, if your group has a lot of goodwill regarding collaboration, you will be well placed to achieve a structured process to get good outcomes from participants.

Step 2: Convene

Bring people together and create the conditions for cocreation

So you've decided to take a collaborative approach. Great! Now you need the right people to come together to make the collaboration possible. The willingness of people to do this, in simple terms, is driven by the value they see in participating. This is their 'value proposition'. Factors that contribute to the value proposition a person perceives can include, but are not limited, to:

1. who the other participants are, and whether the person would like to build relationships with them, or ensure their voice is heard equally

2. opportunities for learning, sharing and influencing outcomes

3. the chance to work on a meaningful project with other interested parties.

With this in mind, step 2 is about:

» selecting the right participants for the collaboration

» determining the collaboration's value proposition

» communicating the value proposition in such a way that you get your participants in the room and ready to participate.

Once you have your stakeholders in the room, ready to kick things off, you'll be able to move on to the next step.

Who should you invite to collaborate?

A useful way of building your understanding of who you should be approaching, and on what premise, is to use the 3Cs framework to develop a stakeholder map. Figure 18 shows how you can organise your participants into three groups according to their level of engagement and the types of activities they will be involved in.

Figure 18: Anatomy of a collaborative community

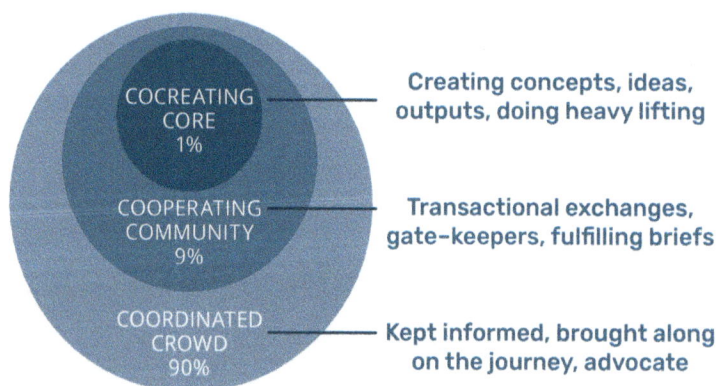

COCREATING CORE 1% — Creating concepts, ideas, outputs, doing heavy lifting

COOPERATING COMMUNITY 9% — Transactional exchanges, gate-keepers, fulfilling briefs

COORDINATED CROWD 90% — Kept informed, brought along on the journey, advocate

Quite often, the primary participants in the cocreating core will be the smallest group, comprising your design and delivery team. These are the people who regularly get together to do the hard work, who do the majority of the decision-making. The next ring out, the cooperating community, involves more-transactional interactions; for example, with suppliers who are fulfilling a brief, or managers who are receiving reports and providing more targeted feedback. Lastly, the coordinated crowd includes any stakeholders not already covered who you need to keep informed along the way, as they might be advocates or brought into the inner circles at a later stage.

Put your participants into three lists either as individuals, groups or organisations. Participants could move between the rings during your project, so just focus on the specific point in time of your collaboration, rather than on the project as a whole. For example, you might invite a wide variety of collaborators early in the process and then become much more selective as you move towards a decision.

Think about how the stakeholders will respond to being asked to participate at the required level. To further determine if you and the stakeholders will both get value from the collaboration, use a double-sided value proposition, as discussed in the next section.

Understanding and positioning the value proposition

A great way to develop and strengthen your understanding of the collaboration requirements is to map out a double-sided value proposition for each participant or group. To do this, simply write down *your* value proposition for involving them (why it's valuable to you to have them involved) and then do the same from their perspective (what value they will gain by participating). This helps you to be more user-centred when you ask people to get involved, connecting to their interests as opposed to just considering your own. When inviting participants, you can literally say, 'I would value your participation for [these reasons], but I also think you might get [this] out of participating. Does this sound right?' This communicates to them that you value their participation and provides an opportunity for feedback on why they feel a collaboration would be beneficial.

Communicating the value proposition

When communicating a value proposition, think about the entire collaboration and the outcome you want to achieve. Using a very simple format such as 'why, how, what, pitch' can help you quickly pull together the information you need to communicate to your participants.

Inspired by Simon Sinek's (2009) widely shared TED talk 'How great leaders inspire action', our approach involves creating three presentation slides worth of content, limiting yourself to a simple title and three supporting points for each slide. These slides serve two purposes. The first is to push you to think through your collaboration more holistically, and the second is to provide useful material you can use in combination with the value propositions to invite participants to join your collaboration.

Your 'why' slide should focus on the deeper value, beliefs and vision your engagement represents. If you aren't sure if you have arrived at this, read your title and ask yourself, 'Why is that important?' Your 'how' slide should describe how your collaboration will achieve its 'why', without letting activities or deliverables slip in (hold on to those for the next step). You might describe the principles that you feel will be critical in realising your vision, or a particular approach that you feel strongly about. Finally, your 'what' slide should focus on the activities that will drive your collaboration. Also try to describe the tangible outputs that will deliver the highest value from the collaboration.

As you start to plan your collaboration, between the above three activities you'll have a map of who to invite, and some material to draw on to justify any resources you need or create compelling invitations to get people to the table.

Step 3: Cocreate

Get people creating together in a variety of settings and under different conditions

The purpose of this step is to unleash your group's collective creative potential and get some work done. It usually has two distinct stages: activities that are designed to build the trust and rapport, and the collaboration itself.

We often refer to the beginning of a collaboration as a 'cold start': it can be hard to get moving. Participants need to build trust and develop a rapport among themselves in order to establish a group identity and an understanding of how they can work together. This provides the momentum needed to deliver your outcomes. You have two main goals here:

» building trust in everyone's motivations (goodwill)

» building trust in the process ('will we really be able to produce something together?').

Once your participants have been primed, you can start your collaboration.

Establishing trust in your collaborators' motivations

To warm things up and start to build trust between participants, you need to create a foundation of shared understanding. A great way to do this is to start your first cocreation session with an activity that prompts participants to share what's important to them regarding the collaboration, and why. This helps everyone understand what is motivating each person to participate, and allows the articulation of the challenges or barriers you need to work through as a group; for example, conflicting priorities.

You can run an activity like this simply by asking each participant to answer a few questions as part of an opening discussion (do this in sub-groups if you're working with more than 10 collaborators, and have each sub-group or a sample of sub-groups report on any commonalities or interesting answers):

1. What is your name [and if relevant], organisation and role?

2. What most interests you about the proposed initiative?

3. What do you see as the biggest challenges and opportunities?

This gives everyone their first chance to contribute and be heard. It also enables them to table any fears they have, which can cause problems later on if they're not expressed. Asking for both positive and negative thoughts helps establish an authentic baseline, as you're not trying to hide the fact that challenges will emerge and need to be addressed – after all, that's why you're there to collaborate.

Establishing trust in getting things done

Beyond trusting each other's motivations, participants need to trust that it's possible to get real work done together. This is important, as many people have had bad experiences of collaboration in the past. Providing a low-risk opportunity for the group to get its feet wet with cocreation can be helpful.

A simple and effective way of doing this is to challenge the group as a whole, or in sub-groups, to build a version of the collaborative outcome using LEGO bricks, or any similar creative medium, such as clay or magazine clippings. This creates a level playing field for contributions, while also pushing participants to prototype elements of the collaboration that they feel are important.[2] It will spur conversations about different aspects of the project, while drawing out the assumptions and expectations held within the group. Because it is done through building blocks, participants take comfort from recognising that there is no expectation that this will be a finished product, only a rapid prototyping experience. That said, it should leave them with a feeling of satisfaction that they can quickly produce something together. This activity should end with a discussion of what it felt like to work together, and what might be learned as you shift into doing the 'real' work. This grounds the exercise so that participants feel like it has a clear purpose in the course of their time together.

Scenario: Using technology in an early collaboration

As you bring your group together, it can be tempting to look to technology to coordinate your work. But while technology such as social media, video-conferencing, wikis and email should certainly be considered as important enablers, in the early stages, be wary of creating too many expectations or requirements for collaborators to use any tools other than what is in the room. Technology can add overheads to participation that can be hard to carry while a group is overcoming its cold start. If you need to use some technology – for example, when a group cannot be in the same physical location – try to find something that participants already use in their day-to-day activities. Beyond this, be guided by the participants' interests in, and attitudes towards, different types of technology. It's important to remember that no matter how perfect a tool might be for a specific job, the adoption of new tools is mostly driven by complex social factors and typically occurs over longer timeframes. So be cautious about bringing anything new into your process too early.

Commencing your collaboration

With trust established among your participants, you can start your collaboration and get that real work done. The way you structure the collaborative process will depend on what you're trying to achieve and the output you're looking for. You might be asking the group to write options for a policy together, or to agree on key issues, or to help you create a plan for engagement throughout your project. Select a technique that you think will suit your purpose.

2   Research 'LEGO Serious Play' for more information on this technique.

A range of techniques is listed in Part Four of this book (see page 97). Among those you might use are:

- » nominal group process
- » community mapping
- » charrette
- » policy wiki
- » citizens' jury
- » ideas challenge
- » codesign process
- » Delphi process
- » search conference.

It's worth doing an analysis before you begin on how the collaboration could go wrong. This means you'll be ready to adapt should a negative scenario arise, with another technique at hand, ready to drill into a specific area. Becoming blocked when trying to untangle and understand a complex issue is a common occurrence. It can absorb a group's time and energy to such a degree that they become bogged down, frustrated, even exasperated. When this happens, it's essential to stop whatever technique you've started, then commence a process that gets the ideas and issues out of the minds of the participants and organised in some type of externalised format. Conversation alone is rarely enough for a group faced with a complex challenge to see a clear path forward.

One simple process is to brainstorm and then, as a first step, capture all the ideas or issues on sticky notes. Now, as a second step, organise the sticky notes into thematic groups. And for the third and final step, explore how these groups relate to one another. Try to show what you want to be taken into the collaboration, and what is important but won't be resolved today. Some people call this the 'car park' – issues that need to be acknowledged but don't have a place in your immediate work. This is an effective process for developing a shared understanding of complex subject matter, or an idea that is still being formed.

If you are facilitating, remain flexible. If the group seems to have a shared understanding, yet the collaboration doesn't seem to be working, you may need to pause to surface and resolve tensions before proceeding (see step 4: Resolve). You may need to do this several times throughout your collaboration in order to get your final output. Getting a great end result sometimes requires a little grit and quick thinking to keep the group out of negative spirals and encourage them to move forward.

Step 4: Resolve

Work through the tensions and challenges that inevitably arise

Once people in a group begin to create with one another, inevitably, tensions will arise. These can come in many forms, such as confusion, frustration, disagreement or disengagement. Dealing with these dynamics is one of the more challenging aspects of collaboration. In fact, a group's ability to constructively recognise, raise and resolve these tensions ultimately determines the quality of its outcomes and overall success.

The key to addressing tension is to recognise that its presence is a natural, even desired part of collaboration. It is not a 'bad' thing to be avoided. Rather, perhaps counterintuitively, the resolution of tension is precisely where collaboration delivers its value. The move from a state of dissonance, when things just don't quite fit together or feel right, to one of consonance, when things seem to click into place, is typically the breakthrough moment – the collective 'Ah-ha!'. When this happens, participants are brought into a greater degree of alignment and shared focus. And often, the greater the dissonance resolved, the greater the consonance achieved, and the greater the value delivered through collaboration. In fact, if you have too little or no tension to resolve, your initiative may be at risk of groupthink – everyone simply nods their heads politely rather than questioning each other and improving their understanding.

Many collaborative groups will have the innate skills to resolve tensions productively – if they're surfaced in a timely and supportive fashion. Most of the time, when tensions cannot be resolved, it's because they haven't been raised early enough in the process. Alternatively, if they are never raised at all, they will reside under the surface of conversations, influencing participation in unproductive ways.

There are two main types of tension, which we discuss next:

1. that which needs to be discussed and dealt with explicitly
2. that which is emotionally based and is usually resolved through the act of being explicitly expressed.

Surfacing tensions to resolve them

A great way of surfacing tensions is a process called 'hearts and elephants'. At the point when tension seems to arise, or even better, at key decision points or milestones before any tension has arisen, simply ask each participant to share what they feel is the 'heart of the matter', as well as the 'elephant in the room'. Ask them to write these down, but allow them to interpret the scope and focus of each question, as this will help them raise the topics that matter most to them. Usually, the group's answers will flag the key tensions that require resolution.

After everyone has shared their 'hearts' and 'elephants', open a conversation about them. If they are written on sticky notes, you might group or otherwise display them, to aid the conversation. Try to get the group to agree which are the most critical, and how to best resolve them.

Surfacing tensions to release underlying emotions

In situations where tension is associated with strong emotions, it's important to provide safe and constructive methods for expressing these emotions. There are a number of 'check-in' techniques that can be used for this purpose (McCarthy & McCarthy, 2002, p. 27). With these, the goal is to give each participant the opportunity to express their feelings, often in relation to a simplified emotional prompt; for example, 'What are you feeling sad/mad/glad about?'. While the replies are being given, other participants are not permitted to comment or interrupt. This provides people with a safe and structured means of sharing, which they can do feeling confident they will be heard, and without fearing that their emotional states will be questioned or criticised. After everyone shares, a discussion can take place about what was heard and what it all means, but which does not name specific participants. Alternatively, after everyone has 'checked in', you can move directly into planning or another activity, whereby the things that still need to be discussed or the perspectives that have changed naturally flow into the process.

Step 5: Maintain

Maintain momentum to keep participants interested, engaged and productive

Depending on the scope of your collaboration, you may need to bring people together a number of times in order to have enough time to develop a solution or understanding. But maintaining a group's interest and commitment after having brought the people together for an initial experience comes with its own challenges.

The requirements for maintaining collaborative momentum are different for each group, mostly depending upon the scope and duration of the challenge the group faces. If your group is likely to need several sessions to complete its work, establish a regular rhythm of cocreation-focused meetings with the 'cocreating core' working group (refer back to Figure 18). This rhythm can be weekly, fortnightly or monthly, depending on your needs. The closer together the meetings are, the easier it will be to build shared working practices and a sense of progress. The people involved in the core group should be those most aligned with coming together to get work done, and keeping the extended stakeholder group coordinated and informed about the process in general.

The core group acts as the engine for enduring collaboration, breaking down hard problems and providing structured, facilitated activities for a larger group of participants. It also makes sure the 'cooperating community' is provided with the right information, at the right time, in the right format, to make their more-transactional contributions – whether they are providers fulfilling a brief or leaders making decisions.

Another critical factor in maintaining momentum, both for your group and the collaboration as a whole, is productivity. While productivity is typically the central goal of collaboration, many factors can slow it down, not least coordinating schedules and participation, resolving tensions, securing resources, and integrating contributions that might come from a wide range of sources. An important part of maintaining productivity is staying focused on the end outcome or output, and continuously prototyping this final 'deliverable' as you go. This will 'bring the future forward', reinforcing for participants the original value proposition, which can get overshadowed by the challenges of staying productive. It will also improve the quality of your outputs by creating more opportunities to gather feedback and make improvements.

Step 6: Grow

Involve more people while maintaining focus and momentum

Akin to the challenge of maintaining momentum and collaboration within a group is growing its membership over time. This is not applicable to most collaborations, but sometimes you will want to expand participation beyond a small group to include hundreds or even thousands of people to deliver impact; for example, crowdsourcing a policy through an online wiki. While it is perhaps one of the most difficult outcomes to deliver in an engagement project, this doesn't mean it's impossible or not a worthy policy goal. Larger collaborations create a movement of champions for your cause.

To support the growth of your collaboration, it's important to:

» be aware of the process and the triggers for growth

» communicate well and regularly

» choose technology that suits your purpose.

Scaling the collaboration

The ability to grow your collaboration to a scale beyond an initial group of 5–10 people is a collective capability that needs to be created. For example, bringing in just one new person can introduce tension and the need to slow down until the new participant is brought up to speed and is contributing productively. New participants may also have input that needs integration. So if you are focused on growing a large group (for example, over 25 participants), you will need to give specific thought to when and how you bring new participants on board.

Collaborations whose memberships do grow see this happen progressively – not necessarily incrementally, but not all at once either. They tend to grow slowly at first but then are able to grow more rapidly the more members have successfully joined. There are several reasons for this. One is that as the group learns what it needs to do to support growth, it can more successfully grow. Another is that growth is also driven by social proof, the dynamic whereby people are attracted to participation because of the participation of others. In other words, simply having more participants will help attract more participants. If you want to scale, use these two dynamics to your advantage.

After letting new members join, pause to review how that process went: What can you use again or improve on? When you're ready to grow again, consider how you can talk about key members or member numbers to encourage new recruits.

Communicating about the collaboration

A critical part of reinforcing social proof, and maintaining momentum, is communicating your activity, progress, and the opportunities to participate. This can take a range of forms, from simple emails and phone calls, through to social media and large-scale promotional campaigns. Keeping this activity consistent and high-quality can be a significant challenge for groups, so make sure it is specifically resourced. When deciding how much resourcing to put behind this function, make it commensurate in some way with the necessity for the group to scale. In other words, the more that involving more participants is a necessary part of your collaboration design, then the more you should resource the outward communications.

Communication activity should be scheduled, as regularity is a key factor. The scheduling can be weekly, fortnightly or monthly, but ideally it will mirror the rhythm of your core group's activity. In addition to a baseline of communications, you should also report any special activities, decisions or outcomes. Promote your activities though the channels that are most relevant to the participants you're hoping to attract, and in a way that demonstrates the value your participants are getting from their involvement. This lets you amplify the social proof your would-be participants need to see to jump on board, and improves the motivation and morale of your core collaborators.

The technology of collaboration

When it comes to scaling collaboration beyond the number of people who can reasonably and regularly fit in a room, technology obviously plays an important role. If you're looking to scale your core group, then you'll need to provide functionality for cocreation – the ability to add to, edit and prune a shared pool of content. This is often in the form of co-authoring documents, spreadsheets and presentations. But it is equally important to consider access to information; for example, sharing an online folder containing all the key documents in order to allow newcomers to get up to speed, build their capability to contribute, and gain a shared understanding of the issues at hand.

The last word on collaboration

The key to good collaboration is summed up by step 1 of the Collabforge method – knowing when you need and want collaboration, and when it's not appropriate.

In Part Four of this book, we provide an overview of numerous engagement techniques, some of which are identified as being useful when you want to collaborate. These can result in great collaborative experiences, but only if you consciously choose and plan your collaboration using the Collabforge method, or by using an equivalent method to guide your collaboration design. Just because a technique *can* be used for collaboration doesn't mean it *will* produce collaboration, not unless you've explicitly planned for it.

4 Engagement techniques

The following techniques are arranged by outcome framework, then alphabetically.

Codesign process

'Ensuring participants feel like they play a part in designing the outcomes'

'Codesign' is a mash-up of 'collaborative' and 'design' and can be used for a range of purposes, including planning for services, products or processes. Codesign is often used as an umbrella term for participatory, cocreating and open design processes.

Codesign processes ensure participants have an equal ability to contribute towards outcomes. Underpinning the idea is that collaborative, cooperative and community-centred approaches to design will lead to more-effective, aligned outcomes.

The key principle of codesign is that we are all 'experts' in regards to our own experiences. This means that anyone who will be affected by, or part of, delivering a policy or service has just as much valuable knowledge to contribute as subject-matter or policy 'experts'.

SCOPE EXPLORE PRIORITISE

DELIBERATE COLLABORATE

LEAD-TIME: 2-3 WEEKS
RUN-TIME: 1-3 DAYS

$2K-10K

3-8

EXPERIENCED FACILITATOR

In 5 steps

1. Establish the purpose of the session with the participants and lay down the ground rules.

2. Have a shared document or plan you are working on as a group to focus on.

3. Ensure all participants have an equal ability to work directly on the plan/document or to contribute through the facilitator.

4. Monitor time carefully to ensure you are able to produce the intended output from the session.

5. Schedule another session if required, or establish protocols to finalise through collaboration outside the session via online or other media.

When to use

This process is best used to make a plan. Involving participants at this stage can generate insights into things that might otherwise disrupt the process; for example, 'It'll need to be closer to public transport', or 'That date is in the school holidays'. It is also used to great effect in solving tough problems – breaking out of internal groupthink can invite creative and fresh approaches.

The value it brings

Immediate benefits

+ Ensures the ideas generated are aligned with stakeholders' needs/interests.

+ Improved knowledge of stakeholder needs.

+ Immediate validation of ideas and concepts.

+ Better cooperation between different people or organisations, and across disciplines.

Long-term benefits

+ Higher degrees of participant satisfaction and trust.

+ Higher-quality, better-aligned solutions

+ Increased levels of support and enthusiasm for the project.

+ Better relationships between the project team and key stakeholders.

Risks to be aware of

+ Codesign empowers participants to have an equal hand in the outcomes. If you are not intending to use the outcomes, make this very clear early on, as this may prompt negative reactions from the group later on.

+ Tensions naturally arise in collaboration. Use a strong facilitator to make sure they can be resolved and the process put back on track.

Tips

Beforehand

+ Find a good facilitator to assist you. Facilitators can gently encourage more-even contribution, and break the power dynamics that naturally occur when participants are familiar with each other or have perceptions of expertise.

+ Carefully select your participants. Because collaboration is hard and requires trust, codesign processes are best undertaken in small groups. Getting the right mix of representation and experience in the room will contribute greatly to the outcomes.

+ Don't expect too much: giving everyone time to talk can make this a lengthy process. Be realistic about what you can achieve in a session, and don't try to tackle more than one or two key outputs.

+ Consider tools that might provide a good focus for outputs. A range of such tools exist, including templates for user journeys, storyboards, prototyping and scenario generation.

During the process

+ Keep a read on the tensions and voices in the room.

+ Be ready to halt the process if a lack of shared terminology or shared understanding is causing tension. This may become evident through body language, an inability to progress, or some participants hesitating to contribute.

Afterwards

+ Once the output of the session is finalised into a shareable form (usually the responsibility of the facilitator or convener), be sure to distribute this to the codesign participants before communicating it more broadly. This ensures that you've correctly interpreted what they've said, and that they feel their experience and knowledge have been valued.

Resources

+ https://www.yacwa.org.au/wp-content/uploads/2016/09/An-Introduction-to-Co-Design-by-Ingrid-Burkett.pdf

+ http://www.smallfire.co.nz/2012/07/04/co-design-workshop-resources-techniques-and-methods/

Collaborative problem definition

'Group scoping and analysis process'

Instead of assuming that the problem you're trying to solve is predetermined, using this technique offers you a way to interrogate the problem itself and collaborate on forming a definition. A group comes together to explore and deeply understand the problem, looking at it from all angles. This builds trust and breaks down tensions, as often the framing of a problem can orient towards particular solutions, putting parties in opposition to it.

SCAN SCOPE

COLLABORATE

LEAD-TIME: 1-2 WEEKS
RUN-TIME: 1-2 DAYS

$1K-20K

3-12

EXPERIENCED FACILITATOR

In 5 steps

1. Convene a group that can offer a diverse range of views and bring different expertise to the table.

2. Begin by discussing what it is that needs to be changed. Try to find a way to phrase this that everyone can agree on.

3. Explore all possible causes, and any data available. Lead a fact-based discussion that is grounded in evidence as much as possible. Record sources of evidence cited by participants for later review.

4. Bring the group back to forming a problem statement. It should be clear and concise, and identify the gap between the current state and the desired state.

5. Record and distribute the agreed problem statement along with any of the evidence cited but not read during the meeting. Allow participants to provide input after the fact if the group isn't fully in agreement by the end of the workshop.

When to use

Collaborative problem definition can be especially helpful in situations of high risk or conflict, as the technique centres on finding shared ground but doesn't require participants to agree on a course of action. In situations where there are competing interests, it can also assist you in learning more about the situation and why certain views are held.

The value it brings

Immediate benefits

+ Builds trust.

+ Enables exploration of causality.

+ Can give opposing groups shared ground.

Long-term benefits

+ Higher-quality, better-aligned solutions.

+ Increased levels of support and enthusiasm for the project.

+ Better relationships between the project team and key stakeholders.

Risks to be aware of

+ If the project is highly divisive, you will want a strong and experienced facilitator to manage tensions and keep the process amicable.

+ If you do not use the problem statement you have created, you will lose trust with the participant groups.

Tips

Beforehand

+ Clearly communicate that you are not looking for answers or solutions in this meeting. People naturally want to solve the problem, so ensure that your expectations are established early on.

During the process

+ If the group is severely divided, continue to push to find the facts on which they can agree. If you can find common ground, it will be easier to build out from there.

+ Have a predetermined format for your problem statement; for example, current state – gap – desired state. Even if you don't use it, it will help centre the discussion when you start asking the group to collaborate on defining the problem.

+ If you're struggling to have the group come to a single problem definition, opt instead to try and gain consensus on either the current state issue facts or the future state opportunity. You may need to write your own statement from this later, but if the group can see their work in it, it is more likely to be accepted.

Afterwards

+ Review all of the cited evidence for accuracy. Some participants may be prone to exaggeration or skewing information to win an argument. If it influenced the outcome, you will want to make sure it meets your expectations before you communicate the problem statement more broadly.

+ If you use a problem statement that you created or edited after the meeting, to retain the trust you've built, send the new statement out to the group for feedback before distributing it to a wider audience.

Resources

+ https://www.oecd.org/pisa/pisaproducts/Draft%20PISA%202015%20Collaborative%20Problem%20Solving%20Framework%20.pdf

+ https://onlinelibrary.wiley.com/doi/abs/10.1111/1467-8691.00157

Advertising

'Quickly getting information to a wide audience'

A method of promotion for key information about a project or other engagement activities. Advertising allows you to reach both specific and broad audiences, depending on your requirements and the media selected. Common media forms include television, newspapers, social media and radio.

While advertising itself is a one-way medium, it can be used as a way of sourcing participants for other engagement activities, such as promoting an event. It can also be useful for announcing an upcoming change, and directing people to information to understand how the change will affect them.

The ability to get a message out to potentially millions of people virtually simultaneously is one of the major appeals of advertising.

COMMUNICATE

SHARE

LEAD-TIME: 6-10 WEEKS
RUN-TIME: 10-40 WEEKS

$5K-100K+

500-2,000+

STRONG COMMUNICATOR

In 5 steps

1. Determine the content you want to communicate.

2. Source an agency or designer to formulate your communication in a way that will get the attention of the audience.

3. Work with the agency or a media buyer to determine the right media and channels for your message. Prior research on the intended audience can be helpful here to know what they are likely to be watching/reading/seeing.

4. Deliver your advertising campaign.

5. Measure your campaign's reach to determine if you have had the intended impact.

When to use advertising

When you need to get a message out to a lot of people quickly and easily. Advertising can let people know about your project or other activities, particularly if you need to get people's attention so that they attend.

The value it brings

Immediate benefits

+ Wide and targeted reach is possible.

+ Advertising channels will be accessible to most people (for example, television).

Long-term benefits

+ If your message was well received, this may have a favourable impact on the perception of your organisation over the longer term (even once your message has been forgotten).

Risks to be aware of

+ A poorly considered campaign could result in negative press or the perception that it was a waste of money.

+ Advertising can be quite costly and is hard to do well on a shoestring, so get good support from design and communication experts. If you have no budget but can't avoid advertising, then keep your message as simple and direct as possible.

+ People will only act on your advertising if it's in their interests to do so. If you miss the mark on messaging and fail to connect with the right motivators, it won't deliver the result you are expecting.

+ Some channels require more notice than others. Television and billboard advertising can be scheduled months in advance, for example.

Tips

Beforehand

+ Set clear goals regarding who and how many people you want to reach. This will help you select the right media channels. Be as specific as you can.

+ Test your advertisement with members of your target audience to check that the language will be understood and the message perceived in the way that you intend.

+ If you're seeking engagement, remember to keep your messaging unbiased.

During the process

+ Keep an eye out on social media for anyone mentioning your advertisement or associated engagements. Be proactive in responding to criticism and address any concerns raised.

Afterwards

+ Reactions and any other coverage that has resulted from your advertising (intentional or not) may be useful in understanding how later policy or service announcements on the same topic will be received, so report on anything significant.

COMMUNICATE

Factsheet

'Visually and concisely communicate information'

A short document (typically 1–2 pages) that concisely and simply conveys the facts of a situation, decision or outcome. Often, factsheets have a visual element to complement the message being communicated. This helps the comprehension of information, especially where the target audience may have varying levels of literacy or English capability.

COMMUNICATE

SHARE

LEAD-TIME: 1-4 WEEKS
RUN-TIME: 12-52 WEEKS

$1K-50K

50-2,000+

STRONG COMMUNICATOR

In 5 steps

1. Determine the outcome required: What do you need users to understand or do after reading your factsheet?

2. Draft the main content for the factsheet.

3. Have a designer finalise the factsheet (if possible), adding visuals, graphs and/or photographs to assist comprehension.

4. Test the factsheet with (ideally) a member of the intended audience to check that the message is properly understood.

5. Update as required before distributing digitally or physically.

When to use

Factsheets can be useful when trying to quickly convey facts in order to garner support, request input, or communicate after a decision has been made. They can be particularly useful in cases where a policy or service is controversial, represents a significant change, or will have a big impact on a group.

The value it brings

Immediate benefits

+ Increased visibility of changes or proposed solutions.

+ Doesn't require any time or effort from the public.

+ Can be low-cost yet high-reach, especially if distributed digitally.

Long-term benefits

+ Improved reception of the final output.

Risks to be aware of

+ Often goes unread unless supported by a good promotional strategy and/or a clear audience need.

+ There is a lack of, or limited opportunities for, feedback, and what feedback there is will require the reader to take additional steps.

Tips

+ Keep the most important information at the top of the factsheet or otherwise prioritise.

+ Spend some time considering the best flow of information with which to tell your story.

+ Put sources in footnotes to avoid cluttering up your precious space.

+ Try to limit each factsheet to the communication of just one message. If there's too much information, consider breaking it up into a series of factsheets or using another format entirely.

+ Make sure your sources are reputable and verify/cross-check as much as possible.

+ Where appropriate, fractions can often be more meaningful/understandable to audiences than percentages; for example, one-third versus 32%.

Resources

+ https://www.thebalancesmb.com/how-to-write-a-fact-sheet-2295946

+ https://ctb.ku.edu/en/table-of-contents/participation/promoting-interest/fact-sheets/main

COMMUNICATE

Free call / 1800 numbers

'Getting information to a broad audience that isn't tech-savvy'

A means for stakeholders to respond to, or have a conversation about, a topic if they have access to a telephone. Typically used in combination with an informational mail-out, this phone service can either be staffed, so that stakeholders can ask and answer questions, or be based on a message service that relies on the caller's keypad or recordings for responses.

COMMUNICATE

SHARE

LEAD-TIME: 2-3 WEEKS
RUN-TIME: 10-40 WEEKS

$10K-100K

500-2,000+

STRONG COMMUNICATOR

In 5 steps

1. Find a service provider (there are agencies that specialise in these services) or arrange a number through your ICT department or phone company.

2. Determine whether you're running an informational campaign or want to capture some feedback from those calling. Create scripts to ask for or provide responses to key questions. If you're staffing your phone lines, you will need to recruit staff and/or provide training.

3. Pre-record material and test the service so that you know how it will work for users. Ideally, also test it with someone who is similar to your target audience, so that you can check that they understand how to work it, and any questions you ask.

4. Advertise or otherwise promote your topic and phone number. This might include anything from targeted mail-outs to social media.

5. Open your phone lines and begin receiving calls. Have a process for recording and tracking statistics you need to measure in the process.

When to use

When you have an audience that is geographically dispersed, with mixed or low technical proficiency or internet access, a free-call informational number can be a good way of enabling an interactive experience for participants.

The value it brings

Immediate benefits

+ Quick way of delivering information or getting feedback.

+ Interactive experience for participants.

+ Participants feel they are being heard.

Long-term benefits

+ Potentially, better alignment of participants with the policy/service outcome.

Risks to be aware of

+ Callers may become frustrated if staff lack key information.

+ Callers may use the service to vent about another related service.

+ Tech-savvy participants may be less inclined to call, preferring to seek information online.

+ Staff motivation can be hard to maintain if most callers are angry or otherwise unhappy.

Tips

Beforehand

+ Consider your options carefully when deciding whether to run this yourself or use a provider. Providers will generally have a call centre where the staff will be taking other calls too. This can mean lower costs, as you aren't paying for the time that they don't spend speaking to the participants. However, these staff will rely much more heavily on scripts and will not be as well versed in the subject matter. You may find you need a mix, where your staff take on the tougher callers and the call centre handles the overflow so callers aren't left waiting too long.

During the process

+ Make sure you have a plan for escalating callers to a senior staff member who is equipped to handle conflict and has a deep understanding of the subject matter.

+ Ensure staff remain courteous and professional at all times. Some level of relating to a caller's situation may be beneficial, but getting too involved or emotional can be problematic.

+ Have daily meetings to bolster the motivation of staff and capture any feedback about questions that are being asked for which they had to go off-script. This will help you to quickly update or provide new information to the team so that callers and staff are not frustrated.

Afterwards

+ If you have a lot of qualitative notes, try to break these up into key sentences and assign a theme to each. This can help you see patterns in seemingly unordered material, so that you can derive the information you need for your engagement project.

COMMUNICATE

Information kit

'A deliberation-support tool'

A selection of carefully chosen information that concisely and simply conveys the facts of a situation. It will include information on both sides of an issue and can be used as a decision-support tool for an audience. It is usually a starting point for research if an individual is motivated to learn more once gaining an overview of a topic. The kit may be a hardcopy or online and contain a range of media as appropriate to the audience.

COMMUNICATE

SHARE

LEAD-TIME: 1-4 WEEKS
RUN-TIME: 12-52 WEEKS

$5K-50K

5-2,000

STRONG COMMUNICATOR

In 5 steps

1. Determine the outcome required: What do you need users to understand or do after reading your information kit?

2. Draft or source and compile the content for the information kit.

3. Have a designer finalise the information kit (if possible), adding visuals, graphs and/or photographs to assist comprehension. This will ensure that both sides of an issue are represented equally.

4. Test the information kit with (ideally) a member of the intended audience to check that the right level of comprehension has been realised and the kit appears unbiased.

5. Update as required before distributing digitally or physically.

When to use

Information kits are useful whenever participants are required to learn about and deliberate on a particular issue. By providing more than one source of information on a topic, and presenting this information in an equitable way, they can help participants understand various perspectives, reducing the bias that news sources and design can bring. They are particularly useful when requesting input from an audience on a topic about which they may have only limited prior knowledge.

The value it brings

Immediate benefits

+ Increased visibility of changes or proposed solutions.

+ Doesn't require any time or effort from the public.

+ Can be low-cost yet high-reach, especially if distributed digitally.

Long-term benefits

+ Improved reception of the final output.

Risks to be aware of

+ Often goes unread unless supported by a good promotional strategy and/or a clear audience need.

+ There is a lack of, or limited opportunities for, feedback, and what feedback there is will require additional steps to be taken by the reader.

Tips

+ Keep the most important information at the top of each page or otherwise prioritised.

+ Consider the best flow of information with which to fairly describe the situation.

+ Put sources in footnotes or otherwise indicate them, to enable readers to follow up with their own research.

+ Make sure your sources are reputable, and verify/cross-check as much as possible.

Interactive e-conferencing

'Electronic public meetings or presentations'

An electronic version of a community or public meeting–style event (see page 124). This conference is usually convened for the benefit of those who are in remote locations or otherwise may not be able to attend a physical meeting. It's usually run with a specific purpose or goal in mind, and while typically informational, it allows plenty of time for participants to ask questions. Any questions may be responded to immediately, or they can be recorded and responded to after the event – often, a combination of the two enables the most participation and allows the conference to keep to time.

Typically, electronic public meetings are advertised in the same way as conventional ones. But there is less capacity for the audience to really get involved, and their ability to gauge the mood of their fellow viewers is limited.

COMMUNICATE

SHARE

LEAD-TIME: 1-4 WEEKS
RUN-TIME: <1 DAYS

$2K-10K

50-2,000+

STRONG COMMUNICATOR

In 5 steps

1. Determine the right software to use. Consider issues – such as the need to download software – that may make people less able to participate.

2. Advertise and promote your event as widely as appropriate. Consider unusual channels such as doctors' offices and post offices – places where your audience may pay more attention to your notice.

3. Start your meeting by communicating a clear purpose and expectation. Ensure that everyone understands what will be discussed and what you are asking of them.

4. Listen to feedback respectfully and thoughtfully. Record for later review.

5. After the event, communicate back through the appropriate channels what you got out of it and how it influenced your project.

When to use

An interactive e-conference public meeting is a great tool for scenarios where you need to provide information to a community group and want to allow the group to ask questions.

The value it brings

Immediate benefits

+ Increased visibility of changes or proposed solutions.

+ Quick feedback.

+ Fast input for decision-making.

+ Lends the voices of key stakeholders to the decision-making process.

+ Lends some transparency to the decision-making process.

+ May raise key risks that have not yet been addressed in the decision documents.

Long-term benefits

+ Improved reception of the final output.

+ Better relationships between the project team and key stakeholders.

Risks to be aware of

+ Those who attend are most likely to be passionate about the topic, so they will not be a representative sample of the broader audience.

+ The ability of participants to provide information or otherwise contribute is highly limited in this format. If you want feedback, plan for this by allowing watchers to vote or submit comments at specific points.

+ Make sure you have controls to mute all participants, particularly if there is a large number whose comments and questions you'll want to restrict to typing only, or one-at-a-time audio.

+ Consider whether it is appropriate for participants to see the comments and questions added by others. This may be a distraction.

+ If you are hosting and reading questions off the screen yourself as they come up, it can be hard to quickly spot duplicate questions, and the audience may end up watching you say 'Answered that one already' again and again. Work with someone else who can process the questions for you to keep things moving.

Tips

Beforehand

+ Consider a series of meetings rather than a single event if you have a lot of information to get through or would like a wider range of individuals to attend.

+ In all the promotional material, clearly and concisely communicate the goal and what attendees will be contributing.

+ Record and post the e-conference on your website so that those who could not attend at the time can still watch and submit their questions within a set time period.

+ Test all technology before the event to ensure that you do not waste any time on this during the meeting.

During the process

+ Allow people to indicate if they are comfortable with their question being read out to other participants.

+ It may be preferable to have a second person summarise questions into generalised questions if you have a great number of people watching. This will avoid the repetition of questions caused by lags, or disruptions if the host needs to recognise that a new question they are reading out is actually a duplicate.

+ Provide an agenda to give structure, and set any ground rules at the start of the meeting.

+ Be flexible. Prepare for a scenario where you do not get through all the material you plan to – discussion almost always takes longer than expected.

Afterwards

+ Summarise and distribute the outcomes, preferably in the same places where you advertised the meeting, so that the community feels like it was heard and its time was respected.

Media event

'Using the media to help spread a message'

Help spread information widely about your new policy or service in a short space of time, using media outlets such as television news. These are typically held when you have something to announce that will affect or interest a large number of people, such as a decision about a policy, or an upcoming public event such as a citizens' jury (see page 154).

COMMUNICATE

SHARE

LEAD-TIME: 1-4 WEEKS
RUN-TIME: <1 DAY

$1K-20K

20-150

STRONG COMMUNICATOR

In 5 steps

1. Determine your key messages and who will be interested in them. Also decide who will be speaking – usually, the more important the person, the more media will attend. Ministers often find themselves the speakers at media events for this reason.

2. Announce your event to the appropriate media contacts, and share through social media if you're happy to also open up the event to the public.

3. Pre-prepare your speaker for answering a range of questions on the topic. Determine how you will handle any conflict that arises if the public is in attendance. And provide a means by which people can learn more in the closing comments.

4. Secure your venue, and if necessary other resources such as catering and/or security personnel.

5. Once your event is complete, monitor social media to gauge the reaction, recording anything important to your process. Respond to questions and comments in a timely and courteous fashion.

When to use

A media event is a great way to communicate an announcement on a new policy or service, or an upcoming call for engagement if your project is high-profile and you want to reach a large number of affected parties with limited effort and cost.

The value it brings

Immediate benefits

+ Quickly reach a broad audience.

+ Increased visibility.

Long-term benefits

+ Reduced conflict when new changes take effect.

Risks to be aware of

+ If what is said is not carefully planned, it might not come across in the way you intend it to. Test your messaging first if possible, or stick to the most conservative and fact-based components of your issue.

+ It's not always possible to predict the result of a public announcement. Prepare in advance for any conflict or backlash that might arise. It's good to pair the announcement with a free-call or 1800 number (see page 106), or to put on extra reception/call staff, to deal with questions from the public.

Tips

Beforehand

+ Research who is likely to attend and what questions they might have, and prepare material accordingly.

+ Ensure your signage is attractive and clearly shows who you represent and the reason you are there.

+ Consider what material you should distribute to attendees and where, or if, the audience can contact you to ask further questions or make comments.

+ Test your content with representatives of the intended audience first. The media likes a scandal, and if they can misinterpret what you say to create conflict, the less-respectable outlets will twist your meaning to get more out of the story.

During the process

+ Have a speaker who is well respected, influential and well briefed.

+ Make sure you have trained your staff to know how to respond when they don't have an answer to a question, and where to direct visitors for further information.

+ Have staff circulate around the event to gauge reactions and note any initial comments or angles regarding your announcement.

Afterwards

+ Be sure to follow up as soon as possible with anyone who provided their details to receive further information.

COMMUNICATE

Press release

'Getting key information to media outlets quickly, using your language'

A summary of the key information you want to distribute, written in a way that makes it easy for the media to reformat your content into articles or news segments. In this way, the media can widely spread information about your new policy or service in a short space of time. Press releases are typically used when you have something to announce, or an event you would like to encourage participation in but which isn't high-profile enough to warrant a media event (see page 112). If your project is high-profile, a press release is often used in conjunction with a media event to ensure consistent messaging, particularly in regards to those news sources that cannot or do not attend your media event.

COMMUNICATE

SHARE

LEAD-TIME: 1-2 WEEKS
RUN-TIME: 1-2 DAYS

$0K-5K

50-2,000

STRONG COMMUNICATOR

In 5 steps

1. Determine your key messages and who will be interested in them. What do you want people to do when they read your information? Ready any supporting material, such as a website or event page, before you send out your release.

2. Distribute your release to the appropriate media contacts. Select those that are the most used by your intended audience, which may include local newspapers or even Facebook page administrators. Reformat the release and also share it through your social media if it makes sense to do so.

3. Be ready to answer a range of questions on the topic. Determine how you will handle any conflict that might arise on social media. Provide a means by which people can learn more about the content.

4. Monitor social media to gauge the reaction, recording anything important to your process.

5. Respond to questions or comments in a timely and courteous fashion.

When to use a press release

A press release is helpful in quickly distributing information to media outlets. It contains your messaging in your desired format, increasing the likelihood that these will reach the public as intended. If picked up and published in the media, they can reach a large segment of your audience with limited effort and cost.

The value it brings

Immediate benefits

+ Quickly reach a broad audience.

+ Increased visibility.

Long-term benefits

+ Reduced conflict when new changes take effect.

Risks to be aware of

+ If what is said is not carefully planned, it might not come across in the way you intend it to. Test your messaging first if possible, or stick to the most conservative and fact-based components of your issue.

+ It's not always possible to predict the results of a press release. If your project is high-profile or contentious, prepare in advance for any conflict or backlash that might arise. It's good to pair the announcement with a free-call or 1800 number (see p. XXX), or to put on extra reception/call staff, to deal with questions from the public.

Tips

+ Research who is likely to be interested and what questions they might have, and prepare material accordingly.

+ First test your content with representatives of the intended audience to ensure you are hitting the mark.

+ Hire interpreters and distribute the release in a range of languages, if appropriate for your audience.

Resources

+ https://coschedule.com/blog/how-to-write-press-releases-examples-templates/

+ https://www.oxfam.org.au/get-involved/campaign-with-us/diy-campaigning/make-your-mark-in-the-media/writing-a-press-release/

COMMUNICATE

Trade show or exhibition

'Finding a captive audience for specific feedback or promotion'

Trade shows and exhibitions gather together large numbers of industry members, customers and/or members of the public into a single location for a fixed period of time, usually a day or two. They typically have a specific theme that brings together exhibitors and attendees who have a shared interest. Generally, a trade show is industry-only, whereas an exhibition is open to the public.

COMMUNICATE

SHARE

LEAD-TIME: 6-10+ WEEKS
RUN-TIME: 1-2 DAYS

$5K-20K

100-2,000

STRONG COMMUNICATOR

In 5 steps

1. Find and contact appropriate events in order to register your attendance, and promote your attendance to all relevant stakeholders.

2. Create marketing and informational material as required for the purpose of the exhibit.

3. Attend the event, communicating with both attendees and other exhibitors as required.

4. Capture data from anyone requesting further information or input into future updates.

5. Send out data and next-step information to those who requested it.

When to use

If you're working on a project that will impact a particular industry or geographic region, trade shows and exhibitions can be a great way of making contact with an engaged audience without the effort of needing to convene them yourself.

Trade shows are good when you need to communicate a change or upcoming call for submissions and want to reach a large number of affected parties with limited effort. The timing is important, however, as these events usually run annually in each location, so their use may be determined by when the event occurs in relation to the decision-making process.

The value it brings

Immediate benefits

+ Easily reaching an audience with specific, similar interests.

+ Increased visibility of changes or proposed solutions.

+ Enables direct dialogue with those affected by a project's outcomes.

Long-term benefits

+ Improved reception of outcomes.

Risks to be aware of

+ Generally, exhibiting is an opportunity to answer questions and communicate information, and therefore it is fairly low-risk. Still, ensure that exhibitors are aware of the boundaries of what they can and cannot say, in order to avoid misrepresenting you or making participants feel they have the ability to contribute to, or impact, outcomes when that may not be the case.

Tips

Beforehand

+ Research who is likely to attend and what questions they might have, and prepare material accordingly.

+ Ensure the signage is attractive and clearly shows who you represent and the reason you are there.

+ Discuss with the organiser where you will be located, and determine if there are other exhibitors you would benefit from being near.

+ Consider what material you would like to give away to participants.

During the process

+ Have staff for your exhibit who are friendly, approachable and well briefed.

+ Make sure you have trained staff to know how to respond when they don't have an answer to a question, and where to direct visitors for further information.

+ Have staff circulate around the show. In some cases, exhibit staff might be just as important to you as attendees.

+ Other exhibit staff may be part of a sales team rather than the intended audience for your message. Try to determine this quickly and provide information for them to take to give to the right person later on.

Afterwards

+ Be sure to follow up as soon as possible with anyone who provided their details for further information.

COMMUNICATE

Bilateral meeting

'Informal discussions to explore distinct perspectives and the rationales behind them'

One-on-one meetings between the government and stakeholder representatives, with the purpose of identifying issues and defining the stakeholder group's perspective and the rationale behind it. Somewhat similar to an interview, but the representative may take the lead on what will be discussed, rather than having an agenda and formal, predetermined questions.

SCAN PRIORITISE

CONSULT

LEAD-TIME: 2-4 WEEKS
RUN-TIME: <1 DAYS

$0K-5K

1-3

STRONG COMMUNICATOR

In 5 steps

1. Invite representatives who hold a distinct view to a meeting. You may need to schedule meetings with their opponents or those who hold other views at the same time, to appear fair.

2. Openly discuss all the aspects of the issue that the representatives want to discuss. A questioning style such as appreciative inquiry can be beneficial, as it comes from the perspective of trying to understand deeply.

3. During the conversation, record any sources provided as evidence for later review.

4. Record or take note of key points and any stakeholders whom the representatives believe feel the same way.

5. Keep a record of which stakeholder groups you have held meetings with, to ensure transparency.

When to use

When you are exploring and seeking information about the issues surrounding your project. It's best to have these conversations early on, before you decide on a course or outcome. Bilateral meetings can be used in high-risk engagements where there are tense relations between opposing groups and collaborative methods are not possible.

The value it brings

Immediate benefits

+ Provides insight into issues.

+ Builds trust with representatives.

+ Ensures all sides can contribute.

Long-term benefits

+ Improved trust.

Risks to be aware of

+ Does not help build bridges between opposing groups.

+ May not be representative of all stakeholders' range of opinions.

+ The loudest voices will get the most attention.

+ May not be inclusive of marginalised stakeholders who are not able to make a strong case for their views.

Tips

Beforehand

+ Complete a stakeholder assessment so you know the groups, their power dynamics, and their position beforehand and can set up meetings with representatives from each.

+ Allow enough time to get in the calendars of all the selected group representatives.

During the process

+ Be as neutral as possible; don't ask leading questions or show an inclination towards a particular outcome.

+ Have meetings face-to-face so that you can analyse unspoken information, such as body language if the person is less sure of their evidence.

Afterwards

+ Thank all representatives for their time and ensure their contributions are recorded in your final report.

SCAN

Citizens' panel

'An established, representative group that can be readily consulted'

A large, demographically representative group of citizens who have been invited to be part of an ongoing program of research and consultation. Participants are generally recruited through random sampling of the electoral roll or postcode address file, and may be available for consultation over a period of months or years. Typically, consultation of the panel involves regular surveys but may extend to focus groups and workshops.

This is not an engagement technique in itself, rather a means of sourcing and maintaining a representative group of citizens who can be easily contacted when the need arises. The clear communication of expectations at the recruitment stage is important in making the citizens' ongoing involvement a positive experience.

SCAN PRIORITISE

CONSULT

LEAD-TIME: 4-6 WEEKS
RUN-TIME: 12-52 WEEKS

$1K-20K

20-100

STRONG COMMUNICATOR

In 5 steps

1. Map out the desirable make-up of a panel.

2. Develop material that presents both a clear value proposition to participants and what their level of commitment will be if they accept.

3. Communicate requests for participation that allow some lead time, so the participant can ensure their availability.

4. Provide feedback on outcomes where appropriate.

5. At the end of the citizens' panel, provide feedback on the sum total impact – the number of policies, services and so on that used the participants' feedback as input.

When to use

This participant recruitment technique is most appropriate in the planning stages of a project, if it's likely that regular ongoing consultation will be required.

The panel can also be used to track changes in participants' attitudes towards certain issues over time. As a result, it may also be useful in the delivery stage as a means of getting targeted feedback to measure the success of implementation.

The value it brings

Immediate benefits

+ Allows the targeting of specific groups.

+ Can enable feedback from a representative sample, even with very short lead times.

Long-term benefits

+ Tracking of the sentiment of a group over time.

+ Building a dialogue between the community and government.

Risks to be aware of

+ Having one group that is repeatedly engaged may limit exposure to new ideas and create false expectations of the actual population's sentiment, especially if the participant group is not large enough to be considered a statistically significant sample.

Tips

Beforehand

+ Determine the sample size and structure you require.

+ Establish documentation and communication paperwork that clearly articulates the task, likely frequency of engagement, and value to the participant.

During the process

+ Ensure that the communication with participants is regular, and that when requests are made, these are done in a consistent and clear manner.

Afterwards

+ If compensation for time is part of the arrangement, ensure that payments are made in a timely manner.

+ Communicate the end results of any projects that participants influence, so that their interest is maintained and they feel like they are having a meaningful impact.

Resources

+ https://www.publicvoice.co.nz/citizens-panel/

Community mapping

'Identifying assets in an area as an input to problem-solving'

Also called asset mapping, this is a process of identifying places, resources and people (assets) in a community that are underutilised, provide an opportunity or otherwise have relevance to a task at hand. This process usually centres on identifying these assets on a map, but can be conducted in person through physically visiting the area, or through discussion around a map.

The process can be particularly useful to designing service delivery programs as it can uncover important allies or physical barriers for the program or recipients. The process should be led with a clear aim in mind, and can be particularly powerful in helping participants feel empowered and connected in designing solutions to their own challenges.

	SCAN
	COLLABORATE
	LEAD-TIME: 1-4 WEEKS RUN-TIME: <1 DAY
	$1K-20K
	5-20
	EXPERIENCED FACILITATOR

In 5 steps

1. Determine how you want participants to indicate assets. This could include travelling through the area to point out assets of interest, discussion around physical map, virtual map, or some combination of these.

2. Invite a range of participants in relation to the challenge at hand. It can be useful to include participants from the general public, specific interest groups, local government, and employees of local services such as libraries etc.

3. Clearly communicate the purpose of the map to participants so they understand what they should be locating for you. At the same time, clarify and define any categories of asset you might be looking for – eg. organisational, associations, individuals, environments/spaces, cultural etc.

4. Through discussion, or other triggers such as walking or storytelling, help participants to identify areas of interest within the community. Record these assets on a map or into an inventory of some sort.

5. Connect assets mapped back to a plan of action. How do each help you achieve your goals? Communicate this plan back to participants. It might be worth checking with them at the same time if your thinking is achievable or realistic.

When to use

A community mapping exercise can be particularly helpful when you need assistance or support of the local community to achieve a goal. Particularly in communities which do not already have a strong sense identity or connection between members.

Community mapping can empower community members to find new, undiscovered ways to solve their own problems. This can reduce dependence of a group on institutions, or shift perception of an institution from seeing that group as a source of problems to being able to provide them with means to help themselves.

The value it brings

Immediate benefits

+ Quickly locate key stakeholders and distribution channels.

+ Improve relationships.

+ Empower problem owners to become problem solvers.

+ Understand potential effects of a policy or service.

Long-term benefits

+ Higher-quality, better-aligned solutions.

+ Increased levels of support and enthusiasm for the project.

+ Better relationships between the project team and key stakeholders.

Risks to be aware of

+ Your map will only be as good as the knowledge of those in the room. Get a mix of people with personal connections, business owners, local government, and deliverers of services to the community.

+ Without focus you could end up with a lot of information which isn't directly helpful to your policy or service design. Be sure to careful craft questions and test these before getting started.

+ Be careful to capture 'why' participants felt an asset was relevant, in addition to the asset itself, or it might not make much sense to you later. It can also be helpful to capture the 'who' too, so you know more about how that asset is being used right now.

+ If you are doing a walk or drive through of an area, ensure that you assess for safety and advise participants of any issues such as road safety, visibility or other hazards in your initial briefing.

Tips

Beforehand

+ For many processes google maps style street maps will work fine. But in more decentralised communities such as rural shires, a more stylised map that features key landmarks may be preferable.

+ If using a physical map, mount it to foam board or similar to allow the use of pins.

+ If running online, consider if you want to enable participants to see and 'agree' or comment on other users' identified assets, or make individual maps.

During the process

+ If using a virtual map, encourage participants to share the map using social media or email sharing tools.

+ Consider recording the discussion. Conversations about specific assets, can be rich in anecdotes or contact names.

+ Keep the focus positive. However, include relevant physical barriers, such as mobile reception blackspots, or areas not served by public transport.

Afterwards

+ Share any report or directory that is generated with the participants. They will often be quite keen to have the information for themselves to make new connections in their community.

Resources

+ http://www.brighterfuturestogether. co.uk/brighter-futures-together-toolkit/ map-assets-in-your-community/

+ https://www.preston.gov.uk/GetAsset. aspx?id=fAAxADMAMQA2ADUA-fAB8AFQAcgB1AGUAfAB8ADAAfAA1

+ http://communitycrewhub.com/assests/ Asset_Mapping_Workbook.pdf

Community or public meeting

'Inviting feedback from community audiences'

A meeting convened with a community with a specific purpose or goal. There is no single format for a public meeting. Some may be more informational, while others may encourage a greater degree of participation from the group. The format of the meeting may be informal or may incorporate other engagement techniques. Typically, public meetings are advertised, have some sort of chairperson or facilitator, and gain feedback from the community on the issue at hand.

SCAN EXPLORE CONFIRM

SHARE CONSULT

LEAD-TIME: 2-4 WEEKS
RUN-TIME: <1 DAY

$1K-20K

20-200

EXPERIENCED FACILITATOR

In 5 steps

1. Decide on and book a location appropriate to your audience. Consider timing that is appropriate for the community to get the highest degree of representation; for example, out of work hours or on a weekend. Consider accessibility and any other factors that might limit attendance and resolve these where possible.

2. Advertise and promote your event as widely as appropriate. Consider unusual channels such as doctors' offices or post offices, places where your audience may pay more attention to your notice.

3. Commence your meeting by communicating a clear purpose and expectation. Ensure that everyone understands what will be discussed and what you are asking of them.

4. Listen and receive feedback respectfully and thoughtfully. Record all feedback for later review.

5. After the event, communicate back through the appropriate channels what you got out of the event and how it influenced your project.

When to use

A community or public meeting is a great tool for scenarios where you need to provide information to a community group and you also seek diverse feedback.

The value it brings

Immediate benefits

+ Increased visibility of changes or proposed solutions.

+ Quick feedback.

+ Fast input for decision-making.

+ Lends the voices of key stakeholders to the decision-making process.

+ Lends some transparency to the decision-making process.

+ May raise key risks that have not yet been addressed in the decision documents.

Long-term benefits

+ Improved reception of the final output.

+ Better relationships between the project team and key stakeholders.

Risks to be aware of

+ Those who attend are most likely to be passionate about the topic, so there will not be a representative sample of the broader audience.

+ Without strong facilitation, the meeting can become focused on negatives or complaints that aren't relevant to your process.

+ Comments from the public often come in the form of long statements. Gently encourage shorter questions, and confirm with those who make statements what their question is before you answer them: 'I understand that what you are asking is whether we will implement this, this year. Is that right?'

Tips

Beforehand

+ Consider a series of meetings rather than a single event if you have a lot of information to get through or would like to create more opportunity for a range of individuals to attend.

+ In all your promotional material, clearly and concisely communicate the goal and what attendees will be contributing.

+ Ensure your venue is a 'neutral' location that does not imply a particular affiliation you do not intend.

+ Test all technology before the event to ensure that you do not waste any time on this during the meeting.

During the process

+ Take photos or videos to share the event with those who cannot attend. Consider live streaming if it is within your budget. However, make allowances for people to opt out of photos/video.

+ Provide an agenda to give the process a structure, and set any ground rules at the start of the meeting.

+ Allow people to vent their frustrations before gently redirecting them back to the purpose of the meeting. Acknowledge anger and then move on to the next person or activity.

+ Be flexible. Prepare for a scenario where you do not get through all the material you planned to – discussion always takes much longer than expected.

Afterwards

+ Summarise and distribute the outcomes, preferably in the same places you advertised the meeting, so the community feels like they were heard and their time was respected.

Resources

+ https://www.epa.gov/international-cooperation/public-participation-guide-public-meetings

+ http://plannersweb.com/2014/10/holding-effective-public-meetings/

SCAN

Consensus conference

'Uncovering points of consensus for better planning and communication'

A deliberative process in which a group of citizens and experts works to develop and describe points of consensus on a particular issue. This may take the form of a report describing the issue in terms, and with facts, on which the participants can agree. It can also be used to generate ideas or deliberate on agreed courses of action.

The consensus conference is similar to a citizens' jury (see page 154) except in that it doesn't seek deliberation on a final course of action. Because there may be multiple points of consensus, the outcome of a consensus conference is less likely to be perceived as a decision-making process, leaving this work for the government or other authority.

A consensus forum (see page 128) follows a similar format, but may include 80–150 people working simultaneously in smaller groups, with the final report being created by the convener.

SCAN	
CONSULT	
LEAD-TIME: 4-6 WEEKS	
RUN-TIME: 2-4 WEEKS	
$5K-$50K	
10-25	
EXPERIENCED FACILITATOR	

In 5 steps

1. Determine the conference make-up and recruit participants. The intent is to involve citizens, and that the mix be representative of the affected community's demographics. When you invite participants, ensure they understand the process and timing.

2. Gather preliminary reading material for the participants. This should cover both sides of the argument and be fact-based. You might also schedule talks or host discussions that further inform the participants prior to the commencement of the conference.

3. Determine the format of the output you're seeking from the participants. Is it centred on particular questions? Will they produce a presentation of key points or a report that consolidates all the agreed-upon material? Who will use the output? This will all help in determining its form.

4. Convene the participants to work together on exploring their points of consensus and building a shared report/output that documents these.

5. Communicate the report to the intended parties, whether this is the public or decision-making parties.

When to use

A consensus conference is useful where there is a lot of conflict over, or misunderstanding about, a topic. The process is about clarification, and this focus on consensus breaks down barriers that might otherwise prevent traction or progress.

The value it brings

Immediate benefits

+ Ability to explore issues or ideas in detail.

+ Direct citizen input into decision-making.

+ Highly focused and detailed discussion.

+ Improved education of citizens on the topic (those participating and attending).

+ Provides a gauge of public opinion.

Long-term benefits

+ Higher degrees of participant satisfaction and trust.

+ Higher-quality, better-aligned solutions.

+ Increased levels of support for outcomes.

Risks to be aware of

+ Because of the small number of participants, the group may not truly reflect or represent the views of the broader population. Consider running more than one conference, or upscaling to a consensus forum if more representation is desirable.

+ The focus on consensus means that difficult discussions around points of contention are avoided, which may lead to key facts or features of the decision being overlooked. This means it's important to balance this input for decision-making with other inputs.

+ The background reading material provided to the group will influence their outputs. If this is not broad enough, or is too complex for participants to understand, the outputs may not be of high quality.

Tips

Beforehand

+ Recruit a group that is as representative as possible of the population it will speak on behalf of.

+ You can include experts among the participants, as long as the ratio is greater than two citizens for every expert.

+ Allow enough time. If your issue is particularly difficult or complex, one day may not be enough to get a consensus, or to find all the points of consensus.

During the process

+ Use strong facilitators to keep the conversation focused on consensus rather than on points of disagreement.

+ Make space for venting, so that participants with strong views feel heard. This will enable them to be ready to start to discuss points of consensus.

+ The structure for how the discussions and consensus-building will be done is not determined by this process. You make take the group through any number of processes during the course of the event in order to build this consensus – this is where the help of an experienced facilitator can be beneficial in planning.

Afterwards

+ Communicate all outcomes back to the participants and any broader interested audience. Include information on how the process affected the decision-makers, so that participants feel like they have had an impact.

Resources

+ https://www.newdemocracy.com.au/consensus-conferences

+ https://participedia.net/en/methods/consensus-conference

+ http://press-files.anu.edu.au/downloads/press/p60381/mobile/ch03s02.html

SCAN

Consensus forum

'Discovering points of consensus across a representative group'

A deliberative process in which a representative, randomly selected group of citizens works alongside experts to develop and describe points of consensus on a particular issue. It can also be used to generate ideas or deliberate on courses of action on which the participants can agree.

The consensus forum is a scaled-up version of a consensus conference, allowing for a more representative range of participants. It differs, however, in that the final report or outputs are compiled by the convening organisation rather than the participants themselves. Like a consensus conference, the outcome is a set of agreed-upon points or courses of action, intended to add information to communications or the decision-making process, but it leaves the process of actual decision-making in the hands of others.

SCAN

CONSULT

LEAD-TIME: 8-16 WEEKS
RUN-TIME: 2-4 WEEKS

$25K-200K

50-150

EXPERIENCED FACILITATOR

In 5 steps

1. Determine the make-up of the conference and recruit participants. The intent is to involve citizens, and that the mix be representative of the affected community's demographics. When you invite participants, ensure they understand the process and timing.

2. Gather preliminary reading material for the participants. This should cover both sides of the argument and be fact-based. You might also schedule talks or host discussions that further inform the participants prior to the commencement of the conference.

3. Determine the format of the output you're seeking from the participants. Is it centred on particular questions? Do you want them to generate ideas or courses of action on which they agree? Who will use the output? This will all help in determining its form.

4. Convene the participants to work together on exploring their points of consensus. While a large number of people may be convened for the day/s of the event, the work will be done in small groups, each led by a facilitator to find the consensus points based on the facts or questions provided.

5. Compile a formal report to communicate the outcome of the forum. Emphasise where points were arrived at by multiple groups, and anything on which all of the forum attendees agreed.

When to use

A consensus forum is useful where there is a lot of conflict or misunderstanding about a topic, and you need to better understand how to get your affected stakeholders to agree, or to communicate well with them during the decision-making process. The process is about clarification, and this focus on consensus will break down barriers that might otherwise prevent traction or progress.

The value it brings

Immediate benefits

+ Ability to explore issues or ideas in detail.

+ Direct citizen input into a decision-making process.

+ Highly focused and detailed discussion.

+ Improved education of citizens on the topic (those participating and attending).

+ Provides a gauge of public opinion.

Long-term benefits

+ Higher degrees of participant satisfaction and trust.

+ Higher-quality, better-aligned solutions.

+ Increased levels of support for outcomes.

Risks to be aware of

+ While a reasonably large number of people can be included, the group may not truly reflect or represent the views of the broader population.

+ The focus on consensus means that difficult discussions around points of contention are avoided, which may lead to key facts or features of the decision being overlooked. This means it's important to balance this input for decision-making with other inputs.

+ The background reading material provided to the group will influence their outputs. If this is not broad enough or is too complex to understand, the outputs may not be of high quality.

Tips

Beforehand

+ Recruit a group that is as representative as possible of the population it will speak on behalf of.

+ You can include experts among the participants, as long as the ratio is greater than two citizens for every expert.

+ Allow enough time. If your issue is particularly difficult or complex, one day may not be enough to get a consensus, or to find all the points of consensus.

During the process

+ Use strong facilitators to keep the conversation focused on consensus rather than on points of disagreement.

+ Make space for venting, so that participants with strong views feel heard. This will enable them to be ready to start to discuss points of consensus.

+ The structure for how the discussions and consensus-building will be done is not determined by this process. You make take the group through any number of processes during the course of the event in order to build this consensus – this is where the help of an experienced facilitator can be beneficial in planning.

+ Look for outcomes from groups that are similar and might be combined into a 'theme' of consensus. In this way, you can determine what participants agreed on without needing the language to be exactly the same. It will also reduce the input to a manageable size.

Afterwards

+ Communicate all outcomes back to the participants and any broader interested audiences. Include information on how the process affected decision-makers, so that participants feel like they have had an impact.

Resources

+ https://participedia.net/en/methods/consensus-forum.

Consultative interview

'One-on-one in-depth discussions'

A one-on-one meeting with a set agenda of questions. Usually, many interviews are conducted and the results compiled to form the overall engagement results. An interview allows for a safe and protected environment where the stakeholder can feel comfortable sharing their views without the influence of others – and without fear of repercussions, as the results are typically anonymised.

Consultative interviews are a good complement to predominantly quantitative engagement techniques such as surveys or polling. They allow you to explore the reasons behind answers and some of the influences that otherwise might not be obvious.

SCAN EXPLORE PRIORITISE

CONSULT

LEAD-TIME: 1-4 WEEKS
RUN-TIME: <1 DAY

$0K-1K

1

STRONG COMMUNICATOR

In 5 steps

1. Determine the purpose of the interviews and who should be interviewed. It could be random or it might relate to another process, such as selecting from those who answered in a particular way in a survey, so that issue can be further explored.

2. Determine your questions. Make sure that these are open-ended and encourage the person to talk, but do not lead them or imply you have an angle on the subject matter.

3. Invite interviewees into the process, ensuring that they are able to get to the venue and be available at a particular time.

4. Conduct your interview. Ensure that you are not disturbed – the interview should take place somewhere the participant feels they can talk without being overheard.

5. Compile your results using a thematic analysis, to make the results of many interviews meaningful to your project.

When to use

When you want to understand a subject's feelings and their reasons for holding a particular view. Interviews can uncover things that aren't observable by an outsider.

The value it brings

Immediate benefits

+ Quick but detailed feedback.

+ Ability to explore the rationale behind views or opinions.

+ Participants are not influenced by others in the room.

+ Allows each participant's voice to carry equal weight.

+ Allows the in-depth discussion of issues.

+ Low to no confrontation.

Long-term benefits

+ Increased understanding of the complexity of local issues.

+ Higher-quality, better-aligned solutions.

+ Better communication involving the public on issues of concern.

Risks to be aware of

+ Your sample size is unlikely to be representational. If a particular aspect becomes influential in the decision-making, ensure that additional quantitative research is completed to confirm the significance of a finding.

+ Can be expensive, as each interviewee may receive compensation for their time.

+ Analysis of results can be time-consuming.

+ The formation of questions can and will affect the results you get. Getting advice from experienced interviewers can be beneficial, to avoid leading participants.

Tips

Beforehand

+ Prioritise your questions. If you can only get through, say, five, decide which are the most important to your output.

+ If a question is particularly important to your process, consider how you can ask it in different ways. This will reduce the chances that the question itself has a correlation to the type of answer you receive.

+ Be prepared to go to participants rather than expecting them to come to you, as this may improve the response rate.

+ Book more interviews than you need – participants regularly drop out at the last minute.

During the process

+ If you plan to record the interview, ensure you have permission first – and a record of that permission. If the interview is anonymous, ensure you do not mention the participant by name after recording starts.

+ Take note of any body language or other cues that may tell you something about how the person feels about an issue or what they are saying. If they don't appear to believe what they are saying, it's important to not go on to your next question but rather to try and reframe your last question, ask related questions, or even directly address their discomfort by asking them if they feel nervous or conflicted.

+ Remain neutral but encouraging in your demeanour throughout the interview.

Afterwards

+ Compile results using a thematic analysis.

+ Provide feedback on what compiled data was used to inform decision-makers and how participants contributed to the process.

Resources

+ https://www.epa.gov/international-coop-eration/public-participation-guide-stake-holder-interviews

+ https://managementhelp.org/businessre-search/interviews.htm

SCAN

Focus group

'Small-group conversations to unpack issues and preferences'

A small-group discussion led by a facilitator. Focus groups are a consultative method that is used to discover preliminary issues that are of concern to a community, or to test ideas and reactions regarding proposed solutions. Additionally, they can help explore concerns that might prevent a proposal from going ahead, or areas that require further research or consultation.

As the group size is small, many focus groups are required to get meaningful or representative results. This technique is best used for fast insights, to be followed up with other methods to improve reach and representation.

SCAN PRIORITISE

CONSULT

LEAD-TIME: 1-4 WEEKS
RUN-TIME: <1 DAY

$4K-10K

4-10

CONFIDENT FACILITATOR

In 5 steps

1. Establish the purpose of the session with the participants and lay down the ground rules. This might include reminding participants about how their information will be anonymised so that they feel comfortable and ready to begin.

2. Try to establish a conversation between the participants that relates to your desired research outcomes. Often, the more spontaneous this conversation, the better the results.

3. Keep track of time, and be ready to gently redirect the conversation when needed to meet outcomes.

4. Make a note of non-verbal cues in the course of the conversation, in addition to what is being said.

5. After completion, identify if there are still unanswered questions, or new questions that have been raised, which should be incorporated into further focus groups.

When to use

Focus groups are most helpful at the beginning and end of a process, with the former focused on quickly getting an understanding of issues and concerns, and the latter supporting the confirmation and/or prioritisation of solutions.

The value it brings

Immediate benefits

+ Quick but detailed feedback.

+ Ability to explore the rationale behind initial reactions.

+ Group interaction forces participants to question their reactions, and shows how social norms can influence outcomes.

+ Allows for the in-depth discussion of issues.

Long-term benefits

+ Increased understanding of the complexity of local issues.

+ Higher-quality, better-aligned solutions.

+ Better communication involving the public on issues of concern.

Risks to be aware of

+ Power dynamics that naturally occur in groups may contribute to some participants tending to take up more air time and swaying the opinions of others. Watch for this and be ready with a strategy to enable more-equal sharing.

+ There may be a lack of representation. Because of the small group size and the power of groupthink dynamics that occurs, your results will be informative but not necessarily fully reflective of the thoughts of the population as a whole. Focus groups are best used as a quickly accessed source of deep information, rather than as evidence for decision-making.

Tips

Beforehand

+ Decide the preferred structure of the focus groups and how many you need to run to achieve your goals.

+ Determine if and how you will compensate participants for their time. Compensation can be an important fåactor in attracting the harder-to-reach groups.

+ Source the participants – you can use marketing research groups to assist with this, or advertise locally.

+ Arrange a time and location that is appropriate for the group's make-up. This may mean meeting out of hours and having a location near easy parking or public transportation.

+ Consider any ethical issues. Also, have questions vetted by an external party or advisory committee to ensure that you're not asking questions that might cause issues, and make sure you have the means of assuring participants that their information will be handled respectfully and safely – particularly if the session is recorded.

During the process

+ Ask participants to be respectful of each other, and to remember that there is no right or wrong answer in this space.

+ Keep the conversation flowing, and try to make sure everyone has an opportunity to speak.

+ Move away from a conversation that is creating conflict if it is not helping to unpack an issue that is critical to your objectives.

Afterwards

+ Follow up by thanking participants for their time and letting them know how they can track the progress of your project.

Resources

+ https://www.citizensadvice.org.uk/Global/CitizensAdvice/Equalities/How%20to%20run%20focus%20groups%20guide.pdf

+ https://mccrindle.com.au/insights/blogarchive/top-10-tips-for-running-focus-groups/

Issues conference

Discussion- and deliberation-focused conference event'

Allows a group of representative individuals to explore and draw conclusions about a topic. It typically runs over one day, commencing with more-information-based sessions in the morning before switching to a format of deliberation or ideation in the afternoon.

The agenda might be predetermined or it can be influenced by the interests of attendees. It is similar to the unconference format (see page 140) but usually involves a goal or outcome the convener wishes to achieve.

SCAN EXPLORE

CONSULT DELIBERATE

LEAD-TIME: 3-6 WEEKS
RUN-TIME: 1-2 DAYS

$10K-40K

20-100

STRONG COMMUNICATOR

In 5 steps

1. Determine who should attend and how you will select and invite them. Decide on the outcome you need from the event and how this will contribute to your process. Do you want the conference to produce prioritised options, for example? Or an analysis of a range of options? Perhaps new ideas, or a risk analysis? Use your outcome to determine what needs to be communicated in the first half of the day, and the format of the afternoon sessions.

2. Determine and invite appropriate speakers who can talk with authority about the subject matter and set the tone for the day.

3. Start the day by setting expectations and providing information and panel talks on a range of themes that relate to your topic. Ensure each explores and opens up the topic, rather than telling participants what they should think.

4. For the second half of the day, plan events that allow participants to break into small groups to analyse specific aspects of the problem that get you closer to your outcome. You can ask participants to self-select for these sessions, allowing them to indicate where they feel they have the most to contribute; for example, 'How this policy might affect young people'. Have a scribe record the key information in each session.

5. Allow ample time to bring everyone back together at the end of the day (or between sessions, if you prefer) to talk about what they discussed, what they learnt, and any ideas or solutions they came up with.

When to use

An issues conference works well in the exploration and prioritisation processes, particularly when focused on a local group or issue. It can help you get a focused discussion on a wide range of aspects of an issue in a short space of time.

The value it brings

Immediate benefits

+ Ability to explore issues or ideas in detail.

+ Enables participants to talk about the things that matter most to them.

+ Quickly provides an indication of issues that might be 'noisy' but which the majority aren't really interested in.

+ Builds trust and relationships between participants.

Long-term benefits

+ Kickstarts local momentum for an issue if ongoing involvement is desirable.

+ Better-aligned solutions and language.

+ Increased levels of support and enthusiasm for the project.

Risks to be aware of

+ If the focus of the conference isn't clear enough, you might not get the information or outputs you're seeking.

+ If the next steps aren't clear or the input isn't well captured, participants may become disillusioned with the process afterwards.

Tips

Beforehand

+ Find a time and location for the event that is appropriate for the audience.

+ Source participants – use local advertising or invite selected experts, and enable them to invite others.

+ Do a site visit and make sure you'll have adequate space for the breakout sessions, while also having a space where the whole group can gather to start and later wrap the day.

During the process

+ Ensure participants understand the 'rules' of the day and feel confident in contributing to each session.

+ Have enough staff so that they can circulate and participate in most breakout sessions. It may be appropriate for your team to act as scribes for the sessions, to make sure that you get the most out of the event.

+ Get everyone together at the end of the day to share the things they learnt and what your next steps are, so participants leave feeling like they have had great conversations and have meaningfully contributed.

Afterwards

+ Follow up with participants by sending them any documents or write-ups that have resulted from the events, and telling them how they can stay involved.

Resources

+ https://participedia.net/en/methods/citizen-conferences

Polling
'Using votes to prioritise options'

This is a process of asking participants for their preference from a range of options. This can be as simple as a yes or no answer to a question, to choosing between dozens of options. Results are usually used as evidence of a broad group's general preference and used as a basis, or justification, for a course of action.

SCAN PRIORITISE CONFIRM

CONSULT

LEAD-TIME: 1-2 WEEKS
RUN-TIME: 1-2 WEEKS

$1K-50K

50-2,000+

STRONG COMMUNICATOR

In 5 steps

1. Determine what you want to achieve, who you need to represent and how the information will be used.

2. Determine the right method for selecting and contacting your audience. Selection could be random, or based on specific characteristics to match your target community. For some groups phone polling might be preferable. In other instances you might be able to use online polling tools to get a quick snapshot.

3. Select your question and answer options, ensuring both are clear and require no interpretation.

4. Open the poll for responses either until you reach you're your required participant breakdown, numbers, or date/time.

5. Communicate poll responses. Many online polls offer an option of showing respondents the results only after the vote, to both encourage them to contribute, and to avoid influencing their input.

When to use

This is best used when you would like to quickly assess the alignment of a large number of people with a potential decision option. Polling can be used in a light and fun way as a part of an in-person event to complement the agenda, or be highly structured as a part of audience research.

The value it brings

Immediate benefits

+ Quick way to test the alignment and/or level of division on a subject.

+ May reach those who would not otherwise engage.

+ Prevents single opinions from appearing representative.

+ Can be simultaneously delivered in multiple languages.

Long-term benefits

+ Higher-quality, better-aligned solutions.

+ Improved trust of outcomes.

Risks to be aware of

+ Because the outcome of polling is generally not binding or influential, responses are less likely to be considered and be subject to a higher number of fake responses – especially when conducted online.

+ May not take into account or surface why participants are voting a particular way, only what their vote is.

+ Online polling through your own website is likely to be significantly biased. Using complementary applications such as google analytics may help to understand what this bias is likely to be, but they should not be considered statistically meaningful.

Tips

Beforehand

+ There are many polling tools out there. Work out the specifications of what you're looking for first before being overwhelmed by the various opportunities.

+ If you need a more statistically relevant poll, contact a market research provider. They are usually able to add a poll into other surveys for a faction of the cost of a whole survey and will be able to help you match very specific target participant characteristics

+ Consider if you need to provide content in multiple languages.

During the process

+ If conducting online, monitor the response to your promotion of the poll and which promotion seems to be working the best. This may also tell you something about the type of bias that can be built into the results; for example, if most of the voters are coming to your tool from a left-wing news source.

Afterwards

+ You will probably not capture information on respondents. If appropriate you might publish an article on the results, or simple post the outcome in the same place as the poll once it is closed.

Resources

+ https://ropercenter.cornell.edu/support/polling-fundamentals/

+ https://bizfluent.com/info-8468866-strengths-weaknesses-scientific-polling.html

Survey

'Quickly turning opinions and data into useful statistics'

Generally, a set of simple questions that enables the creation of statistics. These statistics are used to generalise about how a larger groups feels, acts and thinks regarding a topic or issue. Surveys are a quick and relatively cheap method of consultation, with the biggest cost being sourcing an appropriate sample of the population in order to make the data meaningful.

There are four modes of survey data collection that are commonly used, with selection generally based on the reach and perceived efficacy of the population being surveyed:

+ in-person surveys – the surveyor completes the form for the participant

+ telephone surveys – useful for dispersed populations with mixed digital capability; the surveyor completes the form for the participant

+ self-administered paper-and-pencil surveys – useful for feedback in a physical location, such as 'How did we do?', or as a mail-out to dispersed populations with mixed technical capability

+ self-administered computer surveys – the fastest and cheapest method, but unlikely to produce representative information due to the need for digital capability and equipment.

In 5 steps

1. Determine your research topics. Try to keep these as narrow and focused as possible in order to get the most meaningful data from your survey.

2. Test the survey with a sample group to uncover any issues with the questions or where you might be leading participants.

3. Use a marketing research agency to recruit participants and distribute the surveys.

SCAN PRIORITISE CONFIRM

CONSULT

LEAD-TIME: 2-4 WEEKS
RUN-TIME: 1-2 WEEKS

$1K-50K

20-20,000

STRONG COMMUNICATOR

4. Code each question and answer in order to produce simple reports from the findings.

5. Carefully codify qualitative answers in order to get meaningful results from them, while also keeping an eye out for responses that should be called out separately or quoted, as they address particularly important points.

When to use

Surveys are most useful when you only have a short amount of time and need insights that can be shared as statistics. They can help you better understand an issue or learn more about participant priorities.

As survey outputs are easy to convert into statistics, they are particularly helpful if gathering evidence to provide a rationale for a decision or set of priorities.

The value it brings

Immediate benefits

+ Statistically relevant results.

+ Directly comparable responses.

- Fast evidence-gathering and input for decision-making.

- Better access to time-poor, geographically distant participants.

- Anonymity may improve the honesty of answers.

- Groupthink or power dynamics will not skew the results.

Long-term benefits

- Ability to track changes in sentiment over time.

- Ability to measure outcomes through sentiment changes.

Risks to be aware of

- The questions used in the survey will have the biggest impact on the results. Leading or poorly worded questions will result in outcomes that do not represent actual opinions.

- Statistical relevance will be relative to the size of the sample group. Be cautious regarding how conclusions are made, and be transparent about the limitations of the data.

- Surveys seldom provide 'new' information, as the questions asked rely on the knowledge of the person creating the survey. Surveys are best combined with focus groups both before and after, to improve your understanding of the questions to ask and also uncover what's behind the results.

Tips

Beforehand

- Carefully design and test your survey. It's surprising how often people misunderstand seemingly obvious questions.

- Be very specific about the structure of the sample you need and the number of people you'll be able to reach.

- Choose a delivery method that is appropriate for your participants' needs, your ability to reach them, and the size of the sample.

- Have a plan for how you will use the survey question answers to address your research challenge. Code responses in advance to save time once you receive the results – there are software packages that can assist with this.

- Have a plan for recruiting participants, as advertising might not be enough. You may need to find an agency to source participants; however, there is usually a per-result cost for this.

During the process

- Watch for trends regarding when participants are completing the survey, and extend the time available to contribute responses if need be.

- Make sure you get the right number of results from each demographic group before ending the survey.

Afterwards

- Identify themes in the qualitative data in order to codify and make this feedback more useful to you.

- Allow enough time to analyse the results. The more qualitative questions you have, the longer you'll need.

Resources

- https://blogs.constantcontact.com/how-to-write-survey/

- https://www.surveymonkey.com/mp/survey-guidelines/

Unconference

'Enabling participants to set an agenda and discuss the issues they care most about'

Also known as an 'open space', an event where the agenda is set by those who attend. This can be particularly useful during exploration to surface unexpected topics that are of interest and importance to the community.

The fact that unconferences are participant-led gives these events a different energy, and gives participants a sense of empowerment. Putting the conveners into a listening and hosting role encourages participants to put forward ideas and solutions they may have otherwise held back. This can also be a useful tool for building community momentum on local solutions and events. It enables conversations between those who discover a shared interest through the self-driven agenda, leading to an exchange of knowledge and the building of trust.

SCAN EXPLORE

CONSULT DELIBERATE

LEAD-TIME: 3-6 WEEKS
RUN-TIME: 1-2 DAYS

$10K-40K

20-100

STRONG COMMUNICATOR

In 5 steps

1. Kick things off by discussing the main theme for the day and how an unconference works. Then ask anyone who has a burning issue relevant to the topics at hand to make a session card, come up and introduce it to the group, then add it to a time slot to build the agenda for the unconference.

2. After all the time slots are filled, remind participants of the process principles, where all the allocated spaces are, and announce that the unconference has started.

3. Keep track of time throughout the day, using a bell or other device to make transitions clear. If a group wants to continue through the next time slot, encourage them to move into the shared space instead so that people looking for the next session aren't confused.

4. Check during every session that each group has a scribe, and collect and label outputs at the end of the session for later use.

5. Allow ample time to bring everyone back together at the end of the day (or between sessions, if preferred) to talk about what they discussed, what they learnt, and any ideas or solutions they came up with.

When to use an unconference

Unconferences work best in the exploration and prioritisation processes, particularly when focused on a local group or issue. They can also be a great way of hosting a group of experts. The self-organising format means that you can make the most of the expertise in the room and not rely on expert facilitators.

The value it brings

Immediate benefits

+ Ability to explore issues or ideas in detail.

+ Enables participants to talk about the things that matter most to them.

+ Quickly provides indications of issues that might be 'noisy' but which the majority aren't really interested in.

+ Less planning is required.

+ Builds trust and relationships between participants.

Long-term benefits

+ Kickstarts local momentum on an issue if ongoing involvement is desirable.

+ Better-aligned solutions and language.

+ Increased levels of support and enthusiasm for the project.

Risks to be aware of

+ If the focus of the unconference isn't clear enough, or your facilitator is unable to keep it on track, you might not get the information you're seeking.

+ When the next steps are not clear or the input isn't well captured, participants may become disillusioned with the process.

Tips

Beforehand

+ Decide on a theme for the unconference that will interest participants and inspire them to attend, and come with ideas/ issues to discuss.

+ Find a time and location for the event that is appropriate for the audience.

+ Source participants – use local advertising or invite selected experts, and enable them to invite others.

+ Do a site visit and make sure you'll have adequate space for the breakout sessions, while also having a space where the whole group will be able to gather to plan and wrap the day.

During the process

+ If similar sessions are suggested at the beginning of the day, ask the owners to consider merging or better-differentiating them.

+ Ensure participants understand the 'rules' and feel confident enough to lead or leave a session.

+ Have enough staff that they can circulate and participate in most breakout sessions. It may be appropriate for your team to act as the scribes for the sessions, to make sure that you get the most out of the event.

+ Consider having a visual scribe capture the whole process. This can help participants feel like the seemingly serendipitous conversations are contributing to a meaningful output.

+ Get everyone together at the end of the day to share the things they learnt and what your next steps are, so participants leave feeling that they have had great conversations and have meaningfully contributed.

Afterwards

+ Follow up with participants by sending them any documents or write-ups that have resulted from the events, and telling them how they can stay involved.

Resources

+ http://openspaceworld.org/wp2/what-is/

+ https://medium.com/responsive-org/ how-to-run-an-un-conference-92e7cf089831

Advisory committee, board or council

'Expert advice and ongoing guidance'

A group of appointed persons, established to provide short- or long-term advice on a specific issue or project. The people are typically a diverse mix of stakeholder representatives and subject-matter experts. They may be used to consult on, or collaboratively solve, specific challenges and may also oversee other engagement work being conducted.

Advisory committees, boards or councils bring their own networks of stakeholders to the table, which can benefit a project by providing avenues for engagement or access to hard-to-reach stakeholders. They should be a diverse-enough group to produce helpful tension in the decision-making process and provide fair representation for the project's stakeholders.

EXPLORE PRIORITISE CONFIRM

DELIBERATE

LEAD-TIME: 6-10+ WEEKS
RUN-TIME: 10-40 DAYS

$5K-200K+

5-20

STRONG COMMUNICATOR

In 5 steps

1. Establish a terms-of-reference document that clearly describes the purpose, intent and authority of the advisory committee. This should be explicit enough to provide clear direction, while not prescribing how the committee should achieve its objectives. Importantly, it should state the level of influence the committee will have over the final decision.

2. Begin recruiting your committee. Your selection process and criteria should be openly communicated and transparent. Ensure you get a good, diverse mix of representation on your committee. It can be helpful to include known stakeholders in the selection process to ensure their interests are represented.

3. Host regular meetings to tackle issues that need to be addressed to complete your project.

4. The committee may have the discretion to appoint sub-committees or other persons to undertake pieces of work required by the project (if they have been allocated a budget and the authority to do so).

5. The committee is usually tasked with overseeing the production of a final recommendations document or similar report to mark the end of their role in the project.

When to use

Advisory committees are effective in high-risk engagements where a strong connection to, and collaboration with, the community or interest groups is desirable. They can be beneficial in gaining participation from a broader committee and bringing important specialist knowledge to the table.

The value it brings

Immediate benefits

+ Establishes the principle of collaboration with stakeholders.

+ Enables access to a range of knowledge and expertise.

+ Safe space to develop or test ideas and how they might be perceived by the community.

Long-term benefits

+ Improved reception of the final output.

+ Better relationships between the project team and key stakeholders.

Risks to be aware of

+ May not provide a diverse enough or representative voice if not carefully selected,

+ Likewise, if not carefully vetted, members may be disconnected from the real needs of those they are supposed to represent.

+ Can be expensive if members expect compensation for their time due to the calibre of the individuals often included.

Tips

Beforehand

+ Establish criteria by which you'll select committee members. This might include endorsed expertise in the subject area, strong ties to the community, and a grounded understanding of the systemic relationships.

+ Work with the committee to codesign a code of conduct before they commence. This will ensure everyone has a shared understanding of how they are expected to behave and work together.

+ Provide the information required for decisions or discussion prior to meetings, so that the group can get straight to work.

During the process

+ Commence each meeting by reminding members of their purpose, to help keep them on track.

+ Keep and distribute minutes from each meeting so that members can review them.

+ Use a facilitator or appoint a board chair who can take responsibility for ensuring the committee stays on task.

+ Keep the agenda focused on areas in which the board can have an influence.

Afterwards

+ The names, expertise and affiliations of board members should be included in your final report.

Resources

+ https://www.mosaiclab.com.au/news-all-posts/2017/4/12/8-advisory-committee-challenges-how-to-overcome-them

+ http://www.greaterdandenong.com/document/29503/advisory-committees-and-community-reference-groups

Charrette

'Collaboratively ideating and visually representing solutions'

An intensive collaborative workshop focused on delivering a specific output, often design specifications or concepts. A charrette process requires the prior identification of issues that stakeholders view as priorities. These are used as inputs to enable participants to work together to find, explore and design solutions.

Charrettes are commonly used in urban planning to facilitate input from the community. They are similar to rapid prototyping-type workshops in that they focus on bringing a vision to life through active involvement in generating a solution – often through sketching, mapping or other prototyping techniques.

EXPLORE

DELIBERATE COLLABORATE

LEAD-TIME: 1-4 WEEKS
RUN-TIME: 1-2 DAYS

$2K-25K

8-30

EXPERIENCED FACILITATOR

In 5 steps

1. Establish the purpose of the session with the participants and lay down the ground rules.

2. Have participants work in groups to sketch, make or otherwise design a proposed solution concept.

3. Run multiple 'rounds' of design, giving participants a break between each to reflect on each other's work.

4. Rounds might start from scratch, improve a previous design based on feedback, or build out a new part of the solution, depending on the time available and the outcome required.

5. Try to end with a discussion of the best aspects of all the output ideas, in order to best inform your final design.

When to use

Because of their output and design focus, charrettes are best used in an early phase as an input to implementation plans and/or research proposals. They are especially useful for land-use planning and issues that require speculation about the future.

The value it brings

Immediate benefits

+ Many different ideas and a visual process can spark creative, original solutions.

+ Builds partnerships and positive working relationships with stakeholders.

+ Facilitates efficient decision-making.

+ Fast generation of many design options.

Long-term benefits

+ Higher degree of participant satisfaction and trust.

+ Higher-quality, better-aligned solutions.

+ Increased levels of support and enthusiasm for the project.

+ Better relationships between the project team and key stakeholders.

Risks to be aware of

+ Generally, the output will not be in a final useable form, so communicate that you will be taking all the best ideas, rather than singling out a solution. This will ensure that expectations are set at the right level.

+ If the instructions are not clear enough, participants may feel confused and that their time is being wasted.

Tips

Beforehand

+ Complete scoping and mapping work to discover and prioritise stakeholder issues and key risks.

+ Consider whether a facilitator is required – they are not strictly necessary but are more important for larger groups, or projects with diverse stakeholders, or when conflicts are more likely.

+ Identify the issue the charrette will focus on and key this to one or two central design challenges to get the most useful outcome.

During the process

+ Ensure there is plenty of fuel for the process, both in terms of solid research inputs and food for participants.

+ Try to keep good energy going through regular breaks and check-ins.

+ If conflicts arise, stop and refocus using research – and identify the further research required if going back to the data doesn't help resolve the argument.

Afterwards

+ Once the output of the session is finalised into a shareable form (usually the responsibility of the facilitator or convener), be sure to distribute this to the participants, specifically drawing out where their input was incorporated. Even if you are not inviting specific feedback, this will ensure that participants feel like they have contributed and their time was valued.

Resources

+ https://www.epa.gov/international-cooperation/public-participation-guide-charrettes

+ https://www.nngroup.com/articles/design-charrettes/

Ideas challenge
'Crowdsourcing solutions'

An event conducted either in person or online in which ideas are solicited from a group to solve a specific problem. This can occur over the course of a day or a number of weeks, particularly in the case of online challenges. The ideas submitted are judged by a predetermined set of criteria. There is usually a prize for the winner and some level of commitment to implement the winning idea, or involve it in the final implementation of an initiative.

EXPLORE

DELIBERATE COLLABORATE

LEAD-TIME: 4-8 WEEKS
RUN-TIME: 1-6 WEEKS

$1K-50K

50-2,000+

STRONG COMMUNICATOR

In 5 steps

1. Determine the problem that could use a novel solution and articulate this clearly. Determine the criteria by which ideas will be judged, how ideas will be submitted, and who will judge them. Source the right software or book a venue.

2. Advertise and promote your challenge to those you think might have ideas about how to solve it. Ensure your promotion includes where and when the challenge will take place.

3. Host an opening event where participants can ask clarifying questions and access subject-matter experts or other resources helpful for ideation. These might remain available throughout the challenge, for those who come late.

4. Receive ideas, and clarify with submitters where you do not understand them.

5. Judge ideas. Determine and communicate the intended implementation of the winning idea or idea team.

When to use

An ideas challenge is most useful when you have a tricky problem space that is resisting resolution through more-conventional means. It offers an opportunity to try new thinking and get a grassroots perspective on an issue, which, while will not always providing implementable outcomes, can prompt unexpected solutions to present themselves.

The value it brings

Immediate benefits

+ Fresh thinking about stale problems.

+ Creates excitement around solving a problem in a community.

+ Creates an opportunity for influence for those who are not usually asked.

+ Enables those affected by an issue to architect its solution.

Long-term benefits

+ If ideas are implemented, this can improve the trust by, and connection with, the community.

Risks to be aware of

+ Even a winning idea may not be implementable in its submitted form. Do not expect this technique to solve your problems for you.

+ The judging panel may bring biases that will influence their selection. Ensure diversity in the panel, and have a preset criteria to inform selection.

+ Can be expensive, and the need to provide adequate incentives (often in the form of a cash prize) can block its use in some situations.

+ Not implementing or using a winning idea can degrade trust and interest in future participation.

Tips

Beforehand

+ Provide access to additional resources if the subject is complex or not well known to participants.

+ Procurement of software can take some time. Allow enough time and resources to complete this if your organisation doesn't have a pre-existing arrangement with a supplier.

+ Be as clear as possible in setting expectations for the winning idea. Often, idea submitters aren't interested in being involved in implementation, but some may expect it. Others may expect ongoing ownership or financial reward. Ensure you cover these points and have submitters agree to your terms when they contribute their ideas.

+ Put time and effort into selecting your judging panel. Recruit those responsible for solving the problem and some who are influential with the target audience.

During the process

+ Have a forum for participants to ask questions or clarify the challenge problem. This will help you get results that are more useful for your process.

+ Announcing the winners is an event that can draw attention to your problem space and lend momentum to the next phase of implementation.

Afterwards

+ Communicate not just the winner but how you hope to see the idea realistically contribute to solving the problem.

Resources

+ https://www.viima.com/blog/the-complete-guide-to-idea-challenges

+ https://www.wethinq.com/en/blog/2014/03/18/How-to-Run-Open-Innovation-Challenge.html

+ http://blog.particeep.com/en/innovation-challenge-7-major-steps-on-how-to-do-it/

Policy wiki

'Collaborative online policy editing'

The term 'wiki' is used to describe a piece of software that allows multiple, dispersed authors to edit the content of web pages. This software is used to make collaborative documents, as it allows users to comment on and change one another's text, with strong protocols around visibility of the history of changes and/or versioning. It can also be a database for creating, browsing, changing and searching information (for example, https://wikipedia.org).

Wikis are great tools for building a community and ensuring transparency around the creation or updating of a document. They usually have a range of controls that can mitigate the perceived risk of open collaboration, such as approval workflows, obscenity filters, and the requirement that users create an account and/or be verified.

PRIORITISE CONFIRM

DELIBERATE COLLABORATE

LEAD-TIME: 4-6 WEEKS
RUN-TIME: 4-12 WEEKS

$20K-150K

20-2,000+

STRONG COMMUNICATOR

In 5 steps

1. Publish the wiki, ensuring that the landing page contains clear information as to its purpose, how the final draft will be used, how moderation will work, and any other ground rules.

2. Allow participants to make contributions.

3. Comment on all contributions, integrating as appropriate or providing a reason where an integration is not acceptable.

4. Before the document is finalised, remind key stakeholders to submit comments and changes before the deadline, if they haven't done so already.

5. At the deadline, end the public's ability to edit, but make sure the version history and comments remain visible. Ideally, final edits from decision-makers should be added to this document (either directly or through the project team) in order to have a public record of how the final version was compiled and how contributions were integrated.

When to use

Wikis can be useful in the confirmation stage, to enable feedback and edits in relation to an existing document or piece of policy. However, they can be great for building a document from scratch within a trusted group. When working with the public, having something which is reasonably formed provides a better starting point.

Collaborative document creation can be a lengthy process. If you are pressed for time, this might be appropriate for stakeholders but not for use with the public.

The value it brings

Immediate benefits

+ Enables broad public feedback.

+ Improved transparency of decision-making.

+ Enables feedback from dispersed geographic areas.

+ Allows the loudest opponents/proponents to feel like they have been heard and have contributed.

Long-term benefits

+ Improved reception of the final output.

+ Better-aligned solutions and language.

+ Increased levels of support and enthusiasm for the project.

+ Better relationships between the project team and key stakeholders.

+ Higher degrees of participant satisfaction and trust.

Risks to be aware of

+ A policy wiki requires intensive moderation – if you don't dedicate someone to monitoring and responding to feedback, a few negative interactions between participants can snowball, putting off other participants and, in the worst-case scenario, generating negative press.

+ Lack of representation. If your audience is digitally savvy, wikis can be a great tool. However, if you want a representative sample of a population with diverse technical abilities, you may need to couple this with in-person events, to make sure everyone has the ability to contribute.

Tips

Beforehand

+ Identify a suitable technology partner to host the wiki.

+ Determine a communications strategy, including what the domain name might be and where participants will find information about your project.

+ Plan any security, workflow and user-registration requirements that you need early on.

+ Draft and upload all documents.

During the process

+ Carefully moderate the conversation, including acknowledging and accepting contributions, and rejecting and conscientiously commenting on contributions that aren't suitable.

+ Continue to work on the document as a project team, demonstrating both transparency of process and how you expect others to work.

+ Add comments to your own changes so that participants can see your process in action.

+ Add supporting documents and links to other material as needed, in order to resolve or legitimise decisions and change rejections.

Afterwards

+ Consider adding an acknowledgements section to the final report or document that includes all of the 'authors' who edited the report (you may need to seek their permission first). This will ensure they feel like they were part of the delivery team and had some impact on the outcome.

Resources

+ https://onlinelibrary.wiley.com/doi/full/10.1111/1467-8500.12209

Roundtable

'Facilitated small-group discussion'

A facilitated discussion that gives each participant equal input on a given subject. The table being 'round' alludes to the fact that all members of the discussion should be viewed as contributors of equal value. In practice, a roundtable can involve just one table or many in a room. A facilitator will introduce topics and ensure the flow of the activity. Each table should have a scribe to capture ideas, issues and outcomes.

A roundtable differs from a community or public meeting (see page 124) in that, rather than a broad discussion, it focuses on specific issues to explore solutions, define actions and/or develop strategies. It typically brings together a carefully selected range of people who represent all the perspectives on an issue. The intention is to build relationships and seek consensus between all groups who have an interest in the project's outcomes.

EXPLORE PRIORITISE

CONSULT DELIBERATE

LEAD-TIME: 4–6 WEEKS
RUN-TIME: <1 DAYS

$2K–20K

20–80

EXPERIENCED FACILITATOR

In 5 steps

1. Establish the purpose of the session with the participants and lay down the ground rules.

2. Provide the first discussion topic and define the allocated time and what each table is expected to produce (if anything).

3. Ensure all participants have an equal ability to contribute to the discussion.

4. At the end of the discussion, invite reflections and learnings from the group before moving on to the next topic.

5. At the end of the day, ensure the participants know what your next steps are and how they will be able to review what you produce as a result.

When to use a roundtable

A roundtable is useful when you have a diverse range of stakeholders who don't often have the opportunity to talk to each other, and when your outcomes would benefit from stakeholders increasing their alignment on a topic.

The value it brings

Immediate benefits

+ Access to unexpected and informed ideas and knowledge.

+ Risk identification.

+ Ability to explore the rationale behind reactions.

+ Group interaction forces participants to question their reactions, and shows how social norms might influence outcomes.

+ Allows the in-depth discussion of issues.

Long-term benefits

+ Improved reception of the final output.

+ Better-aligned solutions and language.

+ Increased levels of support and enthusiasm for the project.

+ Better relationships between the project team and key stakeholders.

Risks to be aware of

+ Highly divisive topics can lead to circular discussions that don't produce constructive outcomes. Roundtables are best for topics that are subject to some degree of shared alignment. If you expect tensions, invest in a highly experienced facilitator who can regain control when necessary and redirect the discussion.

Tips

Beforehand

+ Spend a good amount of time determining who needs to be at the event. The right mix of people is critical to the quality of the discussion.

+ Ask the stakeholders who are the most critical to attend first, with options regarding date and time before you lock this in.

+ Plan with plenty of advance notice. Industry leaders and experts tend to be very busy and may need at least 3–4 weeks' notice.

+ Send a reminder a week before the event. This tells everyone to check that your event made it into their calendars and to give you notice if they cannot attend.

During the process

+ If opinions are too divisive, stick to identifying and agreeing on upstream issues rather than solutions.

+ Ensure all parties have an equal opportunity to contribute.

+ If possible, have team members work as scribes on each table to capture information, with your intended outcome in mind.

+ Consider having a visual scribe capture the whole process. This can help participants to feel that the seemingly serendipitous conversations are contributing to a meaningful output.

+ At the end of the day, host a shared discussion to talk about the things that were learnt and what your next steps are, so that participants leave feeling that they have had great conversations and have meaningfully contributed.

Afterwards

+ Follow up with participants by thanking them for their time and sending them any outcomes, as well as a reminder of the next steps for your process, including when the final report/outcome will be made available.

Resources

+ https://www.gevme.com/blog/run-roundtable-meeting/

+ https://www.eventmanagerblog.com/organising-successful-roundtables

Search conference

'Enabling participants to arrive at a shared understanding, strategy and way forward'

An event where thinking and working together takes precedence over learning or listening to experts. This format is useful for complex problems that involve diverse stakeholders, especially if it's necessary for those stakeholders to work together to deliver the eventual solution.

A search conference is similar to an unconference (see page 139) in that it is participant-led and puts the conveners into a listening and hosting role. This fundamental shift can energise participants, and help to deepen mutual understanding and trust, and develop shared values. It goes beyond an unconference because it emphasises arriving at a shared strategy, an agreed solution, and an action plan. Thus, it requires a more structured process and more-active facilitation. The process may need anywhere from 1–3 days, ideally in an immersive situation (that is, away from the usual workplaces and day-to-day concerns).

SCAN EXPLORE PRIORITISE

COLLABORATE

LEAD-TIME: 3-6 WEEKS
RUN-TIME: 1-3 DAYS

$15K- $100K

15-100

EXPERIENCED FACILITATOR

In 5 steps

1. Kick things off by discussing the outcomes and process for the day, and how a search conference works.

2. Focus on developing a shared understanding of the broader system. Encourage many viewpoints, exploratory conversations, and the creation of external visuals that represent the thought process (at a minimum, notes on flip charts).

3. Focus on how the system will change over time. What are the different possible futures? What are our preferred futures? How might we find our way to a preferred future from here?

4. Support the group in developing action plans, roadmaps or implementation plans that can get them to their preferred future.

5. Set up working groups or other ongoing means for participants to deliver on action plans or otherwise make progress together.

When to use

Search conferences are best used when collaboration among participants is crucial to solving the problem and to implementing the solution well. The collaborative approach needs to be well supported by official problem owners, so that participants can trust that their intensive work will have an influence on the outcomes.

The value it brings

Immediate benefits

+ Ability to explore issues or ideas in detail.

+ Enables participants to talk about the things that matter most to them.

+ Can deliver truly novel and high-quality solutions in a short span of time.

+ Builds trust and relationships between participants.

Long-term benefits

+ Kickstarts local momentum on an issue if ongoing involvement is desirable.

+ Better-aligned solutions and language.

+ Increased levels of support and enthusiasm for the project.

Risks to be aware of

+ Planning the event and designing the process is time-consuming and requires specialist expertise.

+ If the process is not sufficiently well designed, or your facilitator is unable to keep it on track, you might not get the result you are seeking.

+ When working groups aren't well supported after the event, or the work is disregarded by decision-makers, participants can become disillusioned with the process.

Tips

Beforehand

+ Clarify the outcomes for the event, and design a process that will deliver those outcomes. Test this with some potential participants.

+ Find a time and location for the event that is appropriate for the audience.

+ Source participants – focus on achieving sufficient diversity to bring all perspectives to the problem: different demographic groups affected by the problem in question, experts from different fields, and participants with different thinking and working styles.

+ Design and plan the working environment carefully to ensure it supports your process, and that participants will be comfortable and relaxed.

During the process

+ Ensure participants understand the process and feel confident enough to express a tension or an idea to improve the process.

+ Have strong facilitators who can keep the process on track, but who also leave room to adapt the process as needed based on what emerges.

+ Avoid any situation where participants are forced to listen to an expert or engage in a learning activity for too long, and focus instead on supporting them to direct their own efforts towards their common goal.

+ Consider having a visual scribe capture the whole process. This can help participants feel like the seemingly serendipitous conversations are contributing to a meaningful output.

+ Have a clear plan for what the post-event work might look like, and how it will be organised and resourced, so that participants have a head start on organising themselves at the end of the event.

Afterwards

+ Follow up with all participants by sending them any documents or write-ups that resulted from the events, and telling them how they can stay involved.

Resources

+ http://actioncatalogue.eu/method/7416

+ http://www.elementsuk.com/libraryofarticles/searchconference.pdf

Citizens' jury

'Enabling a citizen decision-making forum'

Also called a 'planning cell', this is a small group of people who have been carefully selected to match the demographics of a given area. They are convened to deliberate on an issue (generally one clearly framed question) over a period of two to seven days. In addition to the jury, key witnesses are chosen – experts, stakeholders and advocates who represent all sides, which will inform the deliberative process.

Citizens' juries offer a useful tool for engaging citizens on a wide range of issues. They're small enough to allow for effective deliberation, and are relatively inexpensive compared with larger deliberative exercises, such as consensus forums. Participants bring their experiences to the table, and the process can be a useful test run of how the broader public debate on issues may unfold.

PRIORITISE

DELIBERATE COLLABORATE

LEAD-TIME: 6-8 WEEKS
RUN-TIME: 2-4 WEEKS

$1K-20K

20-100

STRONG COMMUNICATOR

In 5 steps

1. Allow the jury a reasonable period of time – as much as a day or two, potentially – to get across the task, any research material, and their own opinions and feelings on the topic.

2. Subsequent days will be split between 'hearings', where expert witnesses explain their perspectives and evidence, and deliberation time.

3. Hearings can be public events if part of the purpose of the jury is to build broader public dialogue and understanding of an issue.

4. A facilitator should remain with the jurors at all stages of deliberation, to ensure that everyone can contribute equally.

5. After a decision is reached, the jury presents their recommendation, the findings/evidence that made the case, and how they came to a decision.

When to use a citizens' jury

Citizens' juries are most applicable if a problem can be solved in a number of ways. The jury explores one or several of these options.

The value it brings

Immediate benefits

+ Ability to explore issues or ideas in detail.

+ Direct citizen input into a decision-making process.

+ Highly focused and detailed discussion.

+ Improved education of citizens on the topic (those participating and attending).

+ Provides a gauge of public opinion.

+ Impartial and objective decision-making process.

Long-term benefits

+ Higher degrees of participant satisfaction and trust.

+ Higher-quality, better-aligned solutions

+ Increased levels of support for outcomes.

Risks to be aware of

+ There is reputation risk if the final decision-makers have a predetermined agenda. If it is not clear that the decision isn't binding, the process may inflame tensions rather than being an outlet for channelling citizen opinions.

Tips

Beforehand

+ Establish a working group and advisory committee to manage tasks and inform the process inputs.

+ Determine how jurors will be selected; for example, a random invitation based on an address in the area.

+ What additional vetting of jurors needs to be done? A survey can quickly assess the appropriateness of a participant.

+ Identify and prepare key 'witnesses' (experts) who will be called upon to present during the process.

+ Communicate clearly to participants and other stakeholders what impact the outcome will have on your project. If the final decision does not lie with the jury, it should be clear how the results will be used to inform the project outcome. Should the outcome not align with the jury's decision, any final report will need to clearly articulate why there was a difference of opinion.

During the process

+ Ensure adequate time is allowed for participants to think, pause and reflect throughout the process; there is often a lot of information to absorb.

+ Ensure that all participants have an equal ability to contribute, whether in questioning processes or deliberations.

Afterwards

+ Ensure that any final report includes information about how the jury process informed the final outcome, and what was learnt that was new as a result. This ensures that even if the decision isn't aligned, participants will not feel like their time was wasted.

Resources

+ https://www.epa.gov/international-co-operation/public-participation-guide-citizen-juries

+ https://www.newdemocracy.com.au/what-is-a-citizens-jury/

Deliberative Polling®[1]

'Smarter, more informed polling of opinions'

A method designed to show how an 'informed' public would feel about an issue. Participants are surveyed before and after participants are given information about an issue and time to deliberate.

This method is typically used with members of the public, with a scientific, representative sample in order to use the results as a guide to what the originating population would think if they had a similar opportunity to deliberate.

SCAN PRIORITISE

CONSULT DELIBERATE

LEAD-TIME: 4-6 WEEKS
RUN-TIME: 1-3 WEEKS

$2K- $10K

20-200

STRONG COMMUNICATOR

In 5 steps

1. Conduct a baseline survey which can be used after the process to analyse how the information provided changed or influenced opinions.

2. Send out briefing materials to participants, including the timing of any additional info sessions. The materials are vetted for balance and accuracy by a balanced advisory group.

3. Allow enough time for participants to consider all the material.

4. Conduct a final survey, and potentially interview participants to understand if and why opinions were changed.

5. Write up the results, focusing particularly on the change between 'before' and 'after', and which messaging was key to the change.

When to use deliberative polling

As a consultative method, this method is often used during planning to inform design, or to present options and understand alignment with proposed solution/s.

Deliberative Polls are particularly informative when you want to engage on complex issues that the public knows little about.

The value it brings

Immediate benefits

+ Enables broad and representative feedback.

+ Improved knowledge of stakeholder needs.

+ May reach those who would not otherwise engage.

+ Can uncover key communications messaging that may be required to educate the public and/or get their buy-in.

+ Identifies the risk of divisive opinions on a topic.

1 Deliberative Polling® is a trademark of James S. Fishkin. Any revenues from the trademark are used to support research at the Center for Deliberative Democracy, Stanford University. More on Deliberative Polling: http://cdd.stanford.edu.

Long-term benefits

+ Increased public understanding of trade-offs and the complexity of the issues.

+ Higher-quality, better-aligned solutions.

+ Better educative communication for the public on issues of concern.

Risks to be aware of

+ Participants have access to information and time that the general public doesn't have access to, this may prove difficult to distribute materials more broadly.

+ While the results of Deliberative Polling are of a representative microcosm of the public, it may be difficult to communicate the results to the rest of the public.

Facilitation

Beforehand

+ Identify and clearly articulate the issue or solution/s you want the participants to consider.

+ Gather or create briefing materials that provide a balanced account of all the information needed for decision-making.

+ Ensure the briefing material is reviewed by an impartial entity or advisory committee, so that the information is accurate and unbiased.

+ Determine the scope for the population that will be measured, and the make-up and size required for a meaningful sample.

+ Communicate the process to participants.

+ Get in touch with key information contacts and schedule events that enable participants to ask questions.

During the process

+ Gather baseline opinion data using surveys or interviews.

+ Distribute briefing materials to participants.

+ Allow participants enough time to read and absorb the briefing materials and attend any planned events (often a week before).

+ Conduct final surveys to record views on the issue/solutions.

Afterwards

+ If not completed during the process, consider interviewing select participants to understand what information was most critical to their opinion, and what (if anything) made them change their opinion.

+ Ensure participants are included in any final distribution of the outcomes, so they understand the impact their input had as part of an overarching decision-making process.

Resources

+ Professor James Fishkin of Stanford University originated the concept of Deliberative Polling® in 1988. You can read more about the technique on the Center for Deliberative Democracy's website http://cdd.stanford.edu/what-is-deliberative-polling/

PRIORITISE

Delphi process

'Consensus-based document creation'

A means of gaining the consensus of experts on a specific issue, often with a future or options orientation. It is coordinated by a facilitator who develops a document through iterations of questionnaires and feedback from subject-matter experts. Experts may be kept anonymous in the process to avoid weighting the feedback of more-influential individuals. The aim is to arrive at a document that explores future scenarios or options and has received the approval of all the experts.

PRIORITISE CONFIRM

CONSULT

LEAD-TIME: 2–4 WEEKS
RUN-TIME: 4–12 WEEKS

$2K– $25K

3–12

STRONG COMMUNICATOR

In 5 steps

1. Determine the issue you want feedback on, being as specific as possible; for example, 'The future impact of a new rail development on the Smalltown commercial district'. Select an appropriate panel of subject-matter experts and a neutral facilitator.

2. Have all the experts anonymously complete a questionnaire that broadly explores the topics. The facilitator should compile a document that draws together the inputs, highlighting where thinking converges or diverges.

3. Based on the aforementioned answers and document, the facilitator should draft and distribute a questionnaire that investigates the next level of detail on the topic, with specific references to possible scenarios or solutions where relevant.

4. Based on all of the answers, the compiled document is updated and distributed to participants for comment. Enabling participants to directly edit sections is worth considering

– ideally, also encourage them to leave a note explaining their rationale for the change, to encourage discussion to resolve differences. A policy wiki–style document can be ideal for this.

5. Over time, each point of disagreement is worked through, with the facilitator being responsible for finding a way to update the document to the satisfaction of all parties. When all participants agree to support the final document, this process has reached a conclusion.

When to use

The Delphi process is great to use when there is a difficult or delicate issue that is not time-sensitive and would benefit from the key parties being aligned regarding possible solutions before these are publicised.

The value it brings

Immediate benefits

+ Lends the voices of key stakeholders to the decision-making process.

+ Lends some transparency to the decision-making process.

+ Access to unexpected and informed ideas and knowledge.

+ Risk identification.

+ Ability to explore the rationale behind initial reactions.

Long-term benefits

+ Improved reception of the final output.

+ Better-aligned solutions and language.

+ Better relationships between the project team and key stakeholders.

Risks to be aware of

+ This process can be very long and time-consuming for a facilitator, who will need to follow up with participants for their feedback during each iteration, and to resolve specific issues that arise.

+ The level of expertise participants have regarding the subject matter will directly impact the quality of the discussion and output.

Tips

Beforehand

+ Understand what technologies or mediums the experts prefer to work in – whether this means online using particular applications, online using email and word-processing applications, or via paper – and plan your time and model accordingly.

+ Give yourself enough time. Experts are often very busy and will only respond to things at the last minute – if at all. Have a strategy in place or incentives that encourage quicker responses, and don't underestimate how long each iteration may take. It's not uncommon for these processes to last 6–12 months or more.

During the process

+ Be patient but firm with participants about timeframes and responses.

Afterwards

+ Be sure to acknowledge the time given to the process and the overall involvement of the expert participants, and the influence the process had on the outcomes.

Resources

+ https://www.projectsmart.co.uk/delphi-technique-a-step-by-step-guide.php

+ https://pareonline.net/pdf/v12n10.pdf

Nominal group process

'Group solution generation, ranking and voting technique'

This technique is a quick and easy to use method to generate and prioritise ideas. It uses individual idea generation to maximise the number of ideas and improve participation from quieter group members. It then uses presentation and dot voting to prioritise ideas and come to a consensus on an outcome.

Not limited to 'idea generation', nominal group process can also be used to clarify key issues, determine budget priorities or build consensus around anything that requires getting from brainstorming to action quickly and easily.

PRIORITISE CONFIRM

CONSULT

LEAD-TIME: 1-4 WEEKS
RUN-TIME: <1 DAY

$2K-20K

5-50

CONFIDENT FACILITATOR

In 5 steps

1. Determine your question. Keep it focused and based in the participants sphere of experience and expertise. For example asking a group of random community members how to improve public transport in their town will result in many ideas that are unfeasible or unviable. Instead focus on something they are an expert on – like their experience, or barriers to taking public transport, which will be more meaningful input for town planners.

2. Ask your participants to brainstorm independently for several minutes in response to your question.

3. Depending on the size of your group, break into sub-groups of 5-6 to present each response in a round-robin style, clustering responses which are the same or similar.

4. Allow time for clarification of the responses. Participants shouldn't comment as to whether the response is good or bad, but instead aim to ensure they fully understand each response.

5. Each participant in the group get a certain number of votes (usually between one and five). These votes are used to determine which responses are most important, to develop consensus on the next step or other outcome.

When to use

Nominal group process is useful when you feel confident that a group has all the knowledge it needs to make a decision, it just needs a small amount of facilitation to gain consensus.

It is most useful at points where there is a limited set of possibilities, but these are in the heads of 'experts', and as such cannot be reviewed, or prioritised. This is often evidenced by circular discussions where you are covering the same or similar ground without resolution. A common example occurs in review processes – determining what could be improved on. As such, nominal group process is commonly used in agile process retrospectives.

The value it brings

Immediate benefits

+ Immediate visibility of ideas, changes, feedback or proposed solutions.

+ Quick feedback.

+ Fast input for decision-making.

+ Reduces circular conversations that go nowhere and disrupt a process.

Long-term benefits

+ Improved reception of the final output.

+ Better relationships between the project team and key stakeholders.

Risks to be aware of

+ Unlike the colloquialism "ask a silly question, you'll get a silly answer", with this process it's all about who you are asking which determines the quality of the question and answers you'll get. To avoid silly answers, keep the question relevant to the participant group. Participants might have different backgrounds, but should have a similar level of expertise, knowledge or capability in the matter at hand.

+ The process can feel overly simplistic. If you are tackling a complex issue using this method, you may want to add in additional steps, such as a second round of brainstorming to take into account ideas generated from other peoples' ideas or perspectives. Alternately you might task groups with researching or assessing the top 5 voted responses, and presenting back before a second round of voting.

+ Because of the need to bring together people with similar levels of expertise, you will need to address a potential lack of diversity within the group – particularly if you are asking them for ideas. Consider who else might have the right level of knowledge but bring a different perspective. For example, in addressing impact of a curriculum change it might be beneficial to invite out-of-school tutors, and school counsellors, in addition to teaching staff.

Tips

Beforehand

+ Consider your question carefully. Will your participants be able to provide input which is viable, feasible and actionable? If not, rework it until you reasonably believe all participants con meaningfully contribute.

During the process

+ Be ready to adjust your process or question if you are not getting the results you need. Be honest about what you need to achieve and ask your participants how you might reframe the question if you are not getting the expected outcome or responses are too vague to be useful.

+ Use the clarify section of the process for yourself as much as anyone else. If you don't understand it, chances are other people won't either, and you could be missing out on an important input.

Afterwards

+ Share any outcomes or actions with participants. If the process has resulted in anything they need to action themselves, be sure to make this clear in follow-up communications.

Resources

+ https://joe.org/joe/1984march/iw2.php

+ https://www.ncbi.nlm.nih.gov/pmc/articles/PMC4909789/

Call for submissions

'Fast, detailed feedback on specific content'

A request made for feedback on a specific document, typically a discussion paper or recommendation report. The call is usually put out to a specific group of key stakeholders, in addition to being made publicly available for comment. The public aspect of the process is often supported by an online portal.

For larger projects, the call for submissions may also be advertised in newspapers or by other means to get attention. Some types of changes have specific requirements as to where these notices must be published. For example, a new building permission may require notification of the planned works and a call for submissions to oppose to be posted at the site and in local newspapers over a period of weeks.

PRIORITISE CONFIRM

CONSULT

LEAD-TIME: 1-2 WEEKS
RUN-TIME: 2-12 WEEKS

$1K-20K

20-2,000+

STRONG COMMUNICATOR

In 5 steps

1. Publish the document you would like feedback on online, or email it to those who are expecting it or have requested it.

2. Advertise the call for submissions as required/desirable.

3. Receive, review and, if appropriate, publish responses.

4. Record the names of respondents and the number of responses for the final report.

5. Review each response for critical changes, risks and general themes in order to provide feedback and input for decision-makers.

When to use

A call for submissions is a consultative method. It is used to confirm that you have correctly understood the issues that a decision will be based on, or to determine the adequacy of, and sentiment regarding, a proposed solution.

Because there is very limited interaction and the publishing of submissions can be controlled, this technique is low-risk and as a result is the most common technique used by governments around the world in decision-making. However, it does not invite new ideas, expand the frame of possibility, or enable representation in response. This means it is not useful for understanding the political context or exploring options.

The value it brings

Immediate benefits

+ Quick feedback.

+ Detailed responses to specific documents.

+ Fast input for decision-making.

+ Lends the voices of key stakeholders to the decision-making process.

+ Lends some transparency to the decision-making process.

+ May raise key risks that have not yet been addressed in the decision documents.

Long-term benefits

+ Improved reception of the final output.

+ Better relationships between the project team and key stakeholders.

Risks to be aware of

+ Submissions may not be in a standard format, and the effort to understand what is of importance in them may be time-consuming and difficult.

+ A select response may mean some critical risks are not adequately identified in the process.

+ Responders representing the interests of citizens may not be in touch with the real issues faced by people who might be affected by the decision.

Tips

Beforehand

+ Consider formatting your document so it includes the questions you would like responders to address, to reduce the time spent analysing responses.

+ Determine how many responses you need to receive to feel that the risks are well identified. Also, make a list of any key parties you need to ensure receive notice of the submission.

+ Consider running another technique, such as surveys, from the same platform to enable participants with differing levels of agency to contribute. Members of the public are likely to shy away from making a formal response to a long and detailed document, not understanding what format of response would be appropriate.

During the process

+ Issue reminders to key stakeholders when closing times are approaching, to ensure all key stakeholders have a chance to contribute.

Afterwards

+ Be sure to accompany any final report to respondents with a note as to how their submission, or the collective submissions, impacted the outcomes.

Computer-assisted participation/democracy

'Using technology to enable citizen voting or self-identification on a spectrum'

Encompasses a number of means for participants to contribute to, or vote on, an outcome using electronic means. It is also called electronic democracy, or decision support systems. Usually, these provide the user with the ability to vote and/or comment on particular outcomes. Some enable users to place themselves on a spectrum rather than give a simple 'yes' or 'no', for a more nuanced view of the group's opinions.

SCAN PRIORITISE CONFIRM

CONSULT DELIBERATE

LEAD-TIME: 4-6 WEEKS
RUN-TIME: 1 DAY - 4 WEEKS

$1K-200K

50-2000+

STRONG COMMUNICATOR

In 5 steps

1. Determine what you want to achieve and the level of influence you are allowing participants to have on the outcomes, so you can select the right technology and clearly communicate limitations and commitments.

2. Select the right technology to get your outcome and set it up with your messaging.

3. If it's a remote event, promote the opportunity to be involved and any time limits on doing so to your audience. If it's being used as part of another in-person event, introduce the technology, allowing enough time for everyone to find or download it – and have a guide in your materials. Let participants know when and for what parts of the event they will use the technology, and who they can ask for help.

4. Monitor behaviour and feedback, ensuring that you manage any conflicts and delete offensive messages.

5. Communicate your outcomes back to participants.

When to use

This is best used when you would like to quickly assess the alignment of a large number of people with a decision outcome. Can be used as a part of an in-person event to complement the agenda, or online and promoted as a stand-alone, self-driven activity.

The value it brings

Immediate benefits

+ Quick way to test the alignment and/or level of division on a subject.

+ May reach those who would not otherwise engage.

+ Prevents single opinions from appearing representative.

+ Can be simultaneously delivered in multiple languages.

Long-term benefits

+ Higher-quality, better-aligned solutions.

+ Improved trust of outcomes.

Risks to be aware of

+ As not everyone is equally digitally able, you will need to pair this technique with others if you are seeking a representative outcome.

+ Can be expensive, especially if users don't have their own devices.

+ May not take into account or surface why participants are voting a particular way, only what their vote is.

+ Fear of new technologies may deter some people from participating.

Tips

Beforehand

+ There are many tools out there. Work out the specifications of what you're looking for first before being overwhelmed by the various opportunities.

+ Set a budget, then work with a provider to meet that budget. Most are willing to negotiate, especially with smaller, values-centric organisations.

+ Test your messaging with some members of your audience. You won't be there to answer questions or course-correct, so you need to know they'll understand both the issue and the ask.

+ Consider if you need to provide content in multiple languages.

During the process

+ Have a strategy for handling offensive input and stick to it. It can be helpful to leave evidence to deter others. For example, rather than deleting a comment, replace it with a label that communicates why it was hidden: 'Comment removed by admin due to not being in the spirit of respectful and generative debate'.

+ Monitor the response to your promotions and which promotion seems to be working the best. This may also tell you something about the type of bias that can be built into the results; for example, if most of the voters are coming to your tool from a left-wing news source.

+ Provide technical support to help users who are struggling to participate.

Afterwards

+ Statistics will be interesting to participants, but also include information on how, or if, the outcomes influenced your project.

Resources

+ https://www.epa.gov/international-cooperation/public-participation-guide-computer-assisted-processes

+ https://www.sciencedirect.com/science/article/pii/S0740624X12000974

CONFIRM

Constituent assembly

An elected representative group determining the drafting of, or changes to, a constitution'

Where a country is governed by a constitution, this can usually only be changed through the formation of a constituent assembly. This is typically a group of citizens elected by a predetermined process and who are convened with a set purpose, such as to amend a specific component of the constitution. The constitution itself should outline the procedure to be undertaken to elect a constituent assembly.

A constituent assembly might also be formed to create a constitution where one does not exist but needs to be created. The intention of the assembly is that it represents the interests of the people (constituents) in drafting and determining the output.

PRIORITISE CONFIRM

COLLABORATE

LEAD-TIME: 26-52 WEEKS
RUN-TIME: 8-26 WEEKS

$2M+

50-150

EXPERIENCED FACILITATOR

In 5 steps

1. Determine the item that needs to be addressed by the assembly and document this in detail.

2. Determine the process by which the constituent assembly will be elected. Arrange any required software or persons who will be required to record the votes of constituents or citizens.

3. Develop and deliver a communications plan to recruit and elect the assembly. This will likely require a range of media, particularly to target groups that might be able to provide electable candidates, such as schools, local persons of note, and community groups.

4. Convene the assembly, providing its members with specific instructions, and arranging and providing input to their decision-making process as required.

5. Communicate the results via the same channels as the original recruitment and election communications.

When to use a constituent assembly

When a constitution needs to be created or amended.

The value it brings

Immediate benefits

+ Allows for changes to foundational legal and governing principles.

Long-term benefits

+ Enables the reform and updating of foundational legal and governing principles over time.

Risks to be aware of

+ Often subject to political or corrupting influences. Have policies and procedures in place to protect against this.

+ A very expensive and lengthy process.

+ May become non-representational if the election process is flawed or key individuals are dissuaded from standing for election.

Tips

Beforehand

+ Ensure that your recruitment, election and process plans align with, and adhere to, any rules set out in the original constitution.

+ Allow significant time and resources for the process. Assume there will be unexpected expenses such as additional research required during the assembly's deliberation.

+ Have a whistleblower policy and procedure in place so that members can raise an alarm if they feel the process has been corrupted by political or other outside pressure.

During the process

+ Monitor the make-up of the assembly. Ensure that a reasonable person would agree that it is representational in its make-up and level of equal contribution to decision-making internally.

+ Be prepared to feed more engagement activities into the assembly's decision-making process. Participants may require specific data to ensure that they feel they are adequately representing constituent opinion.

Afterwards

+ Communicate the outcomes for, and impacts on, existing rules, laws or procedures that may have taken the prior constitution as their foundation.

+ Establish a timeline to update or correct all the affected existing rules, laws or procedures.

Resources

+ http://www.forumcostituzionale. it/wordpress/wp-content/ uploads/2016/06/allegretti_corsi.pdf

+ https://en.wikipedia.org/wiki/ Constituent_assembly

CONFIRM

Additional resources

This book is just a beginning. To continue learning as you get into the thick of planning your engagement, the following websites may be helpful - either to expand your knowledge, provide concrete examples or for inspiration.

Training
IAP2 - https://www.iap2.org.au/Training
DemocracyCo - http://www.democracyco.com.au/our-projects/training/
Capire Learning Labs - https://capire.com.au/communities/learning-labs/

Case studies and/or more engagement activities
Centre for Public Impact - https://www.centreforpublicimpact.org/
Participedia - http://participedia.net/
The Digital Engagement Guide - https://www.digitalengagement.info
Participation Compass - http://participationcompass.org
Place/Matters scenario planning tools - http://bit.ly/placematters-tools
Public Agenda - https://www.publicagenda.org

Lists of tools or providers to support engagement
Scaffle Engage - https://engage.scaffle.com.au/
Participate DB - http://www.participatedb.com
Civic Stack - http://www.civicstack.org
Civic Tech - https://docs.google.com/spreadsheets/d/1FzmvVAKOOFdixCs7oz88cz9g-1fFPHDlg0AHgHCwhf4A/edit#gid=0

For encouragement and inspiration
Engage2Act - https://www.engage2act.org
Cities of Service - https://citiesofservice.org/
#MonthlyMyth MosaicLab - https://www.mosaiclab.com.au/news/
Feedback Labs - https://feedbacklabs.org
Engage Phase - http://engagephase.io/
The GovLab - http://www.thegovlab.org/projects.html
Bang the Table blog - https://www.bangthetable.com/blogs/

For the science and latest research
Journal of Public Deliberation - https://www.publicdeliberation.net/
Ash Centre, Harvard Kennedy School - https://www.innovations.harvard.edu
Engagement Australia, Transform Journal (Education focused) - https://engagementaustralia.org.au/category/transform-journal/

Bibliography

Atlantic Business Magazine, 'The way forward?', 3 January 2018, https://www.atlanticbusinessmagazine.net/article/the-way-forward/

Australian Public Service Commission, 'Tackling wicked problems: A public policy perspective', APSC, 2007, http://www.enablingchange.com.au/wickedproblems.pdf

Cameron, Sarah M, and Ian McAllister, 'Trends in Australian political opinion: Results from the Australian Election Study 1987–2016', School of Politics & International Relations, ANU College of Arts & Social Sciences, December 2016, https://www.australianelectionstudy.org/trends.html

Chevalier, Jacques M, and Daniel J Buckles, 'SAS²: A guide to collaborative inquiry and social engagement', Sage Publications, London, 2008.

Clarke, Robin, 'Valuing dialogue: Economic benefits and social impacts', Sciencewise Expert Resource Centre, August 2015, https://slidelegend.com/valuing-dialogue-economic-benefits-and-social-impacts-science-wise_59ddd62e1723ddf36cfe2733.html

Department of Finance, 'Performance information and indicators', Australian Government, 2010, https://www.finance.gov.au/sites/default/files/performance-information-and-indicators.pdf

Department of Finance, 'Delivering Australian Government services: Access and distribution strategy – Australian Government Service Delivery Framework', Australian Government, 2006, https://www.finance.gov.au/publications/delivering-australian-government-services-access-and-dis-tribution-strategy/framework.html

Department of the Prime Minister and Cabinet, 'Open Government Partnership Australia', Australian Government, 2018, https://ogpau.pmc.gov.au/about-ogp

Government of Newfoundland and Labrador, 'Our fiscal future: Starting the conversation', Newfoundland Labrador, 2018, https://www.gov.nl.ca/OurFiscalFuture/index.html

IAP2 International Federation, 'IAP2's Public Participation Spectrum', International Association for Public Participation, 2014, https://www.iap2.org.au/Tenant/C0000004/00000001/files/IAP2_Public_Participation_Spectrum.pdf

Mayers, James, 'Stakeholder power analysis', International Institute for Environmental Development, March 2005, http://www.policy-power-tools.org/Tools/Understanding/docs/stakeholder_power_tool_english.pdf

McCarthy, Jim, and Michele McCarthy, *Software for Your Head: Core Protocols for Creating and Maintaining Shared Vision*, Addison-Wesley, Boston, 2002.

Naidoo, Merle, 'A situational analysis on the public participation processes in integrated water resources management in the Kat River Valley, Eastern Cape, South Africa', Master's thesis, University of Tokyo, 2009, https://www.researchgate.net/publication/43408341_A_situational_ analysis_on_the_public_participation_processes_in_integrated_water_ resources_management_in_the_Kat_River_Valley_Eastern_Cape_South_ Africa

Office of Best Practice Regulation, 'Australian Government RIS Preliminary Assessment Form: Is a RIS required?', Department of the Prime Minister and Cabinet, Australian Government, 2017, https://www.pmc. gov.au/resource-centre/regulation/australian-government-ris-prelimi- nary-assessment-form-ris-required

Office of Citizens and Civics, 'Working together: Involving community and stakeholders in decision-making', Department of the Premier and Cabinet, Western Australian Government, 2006, http://www.nrm. wa.gov.au/media/10536/working_together_involving_community_and_ stakeholders.pdf

Organisation for Economic Co-operation and Development, *Promise and Problems of E-Democracy: Challenges of Online Citizen Engagement*, Emerging Economies Transition, OECD, Paris, 2003.

Parsons, Jon, 'The cocktail circuit and democracy in N.L.', *The Independent*, 3 November 2016, http://theindependent.ca/2016/11/03/the-cocktail-cir- cuit-and-democracy-in-n-l/

Rollmann, Hans, 'Liberals' austerity budget will hit most vulnerable hardest', *The Independent*, 15 April 2016, http://theindependent.ca/2016/04/15/ liberals-austerity-budget-will-hit-most-vulnerable-hardest/

Roseke, Bernie. 2015. "Checklists of Potential Project Risks." http://www. projectengineer.net/checklist-of-potential-project-risks/.

Ross, Helen, Claudia Baldwin, and RW Carter, 'Subtle implications: Public participation versus community engagement in environmental deci- sion-making', *Australasian Journal of Environmental Management*, vol. 23, no. 2, 2016, pp. 123–9, https://www.tandfonline.com/doi/full/10.1080/1 4486563.2016.1194588

Sheedy, Amanda, 'Handbook on citizen engagement: Beyond consultation', Canadian Policy Research Networks, March 2008, https:// ccednet-rcdec.ca/sites/ccednet-rcdec.ca/files/handbook_on_citizen_ engagement.pdf

Shergold, Peter, 'Learning from failure: Why large government policy initiatives have gone so badly wrong in the past and how the chances of success in the future can be improved', Australian Public Service Commission, 2015, https://www.apsc.gov.au/learning-failure-why-large-government policy-initiatives-have-gone-so-badly-wrong-past-and-how

Sinek, Simon, 'How great leaders inspire action', TED, September 2009, https://www.ted.com/talks/simon_sinek_how_great_leaders_inspire_ action?nolanguage=en%2C+Sept+2009

State of Victoria, Department of Sustainability and Environment. 2005. "Effective Engagement: Building Relationship with Community and Other Stakeholders." The Community Engagement Network.

Stewart, Jenny, *Dilemmas of Engagement: The Role of Consultation in Governance*, ANU Press, Acton, Canberra, 2009, https://press.anu.edu.au/ publications/series/australia-and-new-zealand-school-government- anzsog/dilemmas-engagement

Victorian Local Governance Association, 'Local government consultation and engagement: Definitions', Melbourne, 2018, http://vlgaconsultation.org. au/definitons

Wilson, Zoe, and Sylvain R. Perret. 2009. Social Participation in Water Governance and Management Critical and Global Perspectives. Routledge.

Acknowledgements

Engagement and consultation is, in many ways, still an emerging field. So many amazing people have and are working in this space to enrich democracy and decision making at all levels. The world is a better place due to the work of the academics and dedicated professionals who strive to improve dialogue and collaboration in decision making processes. Thank you all. It is challenging, but important work, making more voices not only heard, but helpful. It is my best hope that this book helps practitioners make better use of your fine works.

This book is written predominantly from the 'we' perspective of Collabforge. This is because it is fundamentally derived from the collective experience I've gained working with Mark Elliott and Hailey Cooperrider both throughout the broader Scaffle development project, and many projects in the years prior. New and old ideas and concepts are rigorously investigated and tested in our collaborations, before we spin them back into new projects such as this book. Hailey & Mark, I've learnt to love, appreciate and rely on working with equal measures of challenge, empathy and inspiration. It's been a tremendous privilege to spreadhead this corner of our research. Thank you for your encouragement to take this on and checking my thinking along the journey.

Scaffle and all the associated research would not have been possible without the Business, Research and Innovation Initiative grant (BRII), sponsored by the Department of Industry, Innovation, and Science. While the grant bought us the opportunity to explore the engagement space, many of the conclusions relied on the significant investment of time from the BRII team. Thank you for always being ready to answer our questions, source interviewees, and test our thinking. Specifically, Iain Kendal for patiently responding to our many emails and providing invaluable feedback on various drafts, Michael Vickers and Damian Carmichael for always asking us the hardest questions, Debbie Mattiuzzo for being so quick to answer questions and connecting us to people who could help, and the whole team for all your feedback and efforts.

Part editor, part coach and part counsellor, I'd like to thank Paul Smitz, for keeping me on track with good humour and a strong sense of timing. It was my first experience writing and the book was strengthened with each interaction. From instilling clear direction in the beginning, to preventing me from constantly hedging, your help was invaluable in getting to this point. Thank you for sharing your patience and experience with me.

It's been a lot of fun working on Scaffle, both the book and the software, particularly because of the people involved and everything they brought to the process. Sophia Ashraf and Frances Gamble, thank you for persevering in pulling together research behind the included engagement techniques. The team at Cogent: Eli Mydiarz, Will Rockel, James Dowling, Matt Ensor, Scott Rogers, and Corrie Butcher, thank you for bringing your humour, processes and questions. The process of working on the application revealed many important lines of inquiry and tested my thinking constantly.

Lastly, my dear husband. Thank you for your patience and endless support. You have a way of helping me believe in myself and keep on keeping on. I appreciate all the meals you cooked and tantrums (mostly our daughter's) that you weathered for me. And thank you little Isabella for being so patient and inspiring me to be my best. I am so lucky and grateful to have you both with me on this journey.